Full-time RV Living

What I Wish I Had Known 7 Years Ago, Before I Hit the Road

By Jerry Minchey

www.LifeRV.com

Stony River Media

Minchey, Jerry. Frugal RVing / Jerry Minchey 2019.02

ISBN-13: 978-1-947020-09-2

1. Retirement living.

Published by Stony River Media

Knoxville, TN

StonyRiverMedia.com

Disclaimer

The information in this book is based on the author's knowledge, experience, and opinions. The methods described in this book are not intended to be a definitive set of instructions. You may discover other methods and materials to accomplish the same result. Your results may differ.

There are no representations or warranties, express or implied, about the completeness, accuracy or reliability of the information, products, services or related materials contained in this book. The information is provided "as is", to be used at your own risk.

This book is not intended to give legal or financial advice and is sold with the understanding that the author is not engaged in rendering legal, accounting, or other professional services or advice. If legal or financial advice or other expert assistance is required, the services of a competent professional should be sought to ensure you fully understand your obligations and risks.

This book includes information regarding the products and services of third parties. I do not assume responsibility for any third-party materials or opinions. Use of mentioned

Version 2019.02

Dedicated to my parents, Charles and Helen Minchey, who taught me to enjoy retirement living.

Table of Contents

Introduction

"Quit your job, buy a ticket, get a tan, fall in love, never return."

~ Anonymous

Does this quote speak to you? It's possible to do this, you know. The best part is that if you have an RV, you don't even have to buy a ticket. All you have to do is get in your RV and go.

I've learned a lot about living full time in an RV during the seven years I've been on the road. I've learned about my RV, about the lifestyle, and I've learned a lot about myself.

I've also learned that the open road is a hard teacher. The test comes first, and the lesson comes later. That's another way of describing the concept of learning things the hard way. I learned a lot about RVing the hard way.

In this book I'm going to share with you the things I learned the hard way. I call them the things I wish I had known before I started RVing.

I now know what I like, what I don't like, and, most of all, I've learned how to relax and enjoy life. I enjoy the beauty and solitude of the mountains when I'm boondocking, and

I enjoy the serendipity of the chance happenings when I'm traveling through small towns that are off the beaten path.

This is a unique time in history

Never has it been so easy to hit the road, live in an RV, and make a living while living this wonderful, adventurous life. You could say because of technology, the economy, and attitudes, it's easier to live-full-time in an RV now than ever before. Maybe that's why over 1,000 RVs are being sold every day.

You could say it's like a perfect storm when everything comes together at the same time, but the difference is that *The Perfect Storm* book and movie described events that took place for only a short time. I can see the RVing version of the perfect storm going on indefinitely and getting even more popular.

Living full time in an RV is no longer just for retired people. One recent industry report said that 40% of the new RVs being sold today are being bought by young, non-retired people.

It's mainly because they can live this low-cost, exciting lifestyle and still make a living on the road.

Can you afford to live full time in an RV?

The simple answer is yes, you can. Your next question is likely to be, how? Just accept this answer for now and keep reading. After all, it doesn't matter if you can afford to do it or how you would go about it until you have a burning desire and decide that you really want to live full time in an RV.

That's why I put off until Chapter 15 discussing how you can make a living on the road. Just accept that it can easily be done and continue reading and decide if you really want to live the full-time RVing lifestyle.

One thing to be prepared for is that things are always going to break. Whether you have a new rig or an old one, it doesn't matter. In fact, believe it or not, in most cases, more things will go wrong with a new RV than with an old one. I'll go into that later.

I don't mind it too much when something breaks that I know is going to wear out sooner or later. For example, I had my fresh water pump stop working recently. I knew that those go out all the time. I had even considered buying a new one and keeping it as a spare so I would have it when it did fail.

What I don't like is when I have to spend money on something that shouldn't wear out. Not long after I bought my motorhome, seven years ago, I noticed that the right side was always sitting lower than the left side. I had to replace the leaf springs on the front and the back on the right side. That was a cost of about $1,800. That's not something that should go bad.

Of course, I've learned a lot about driving, taking care of the things on the RV, and about RV maintenance in general.

I've learned by reading books, watching YouTube videos, and from fellow RVers. Unfortunately, I've also learned a lot of things the hard way.

Hopefully, after reading this book there will be far fewer things you will have to learn the hard way.

Music tells the story when it comes to RVing

There have been a lot of country songs written about the joys of being on the road. Two that come to mind are:

"I've Been Everywhere" sung by Johnny Cash

https://www.youtube.com/watch?v=G536Mb9RsUQ

and

"On the Road Again" by Willie Nelson

https://www.youtube.com/watch?v=Gdlyi5mckg0

You can't listen to these songs without getting the itch to get on the road and go somewhere.

You don't have to stop and listen to these songs right now, but if you do, I think they will get you in the mood to consider the RVing lifestyle.

If you're reading the eBook version, all you have to do is click on the links I've provided, but if you're reading the print version, you have to type the URL into your computer. The good news is that you don't have to type the whole URL.

You can just start typing with the word, "YouTube. . ." You can omit the https://www. part of the URL.

Of course, not all country songs about being on the road are about wanting to go somewhere. Grandpa Jones wrote the song "Eight More Miles to Louisville" about the joy of getting back home. Even though Grandpa Jones wrote and recorded the song, I like Sam Bush's recording of it better.

"Eight More Miles to Louisville" by Sam Bush

https://www.youtube.com/watch?v=uMIMKSlLsqM

And of course, the best song of all time about getting back home (in my opinion) is . . .

"Take me Home Country Roads" by John Denver

https://www.youtube.com/watch?v=IUmnTfsY3hI

That's enough songs about getting back home. If you listen to many of these kinds of songs, you might decide that you don't want to get on the road in your RV, so let's get to fun songs about being on the road in an RV.

Here are two of my favorite songs about RV life on the road.

"Home Sweet Home in My RV" by Roger Hurricane Wilson

https://www.youtube.com/watch?v=bFd1r56De2o

and

"My Home" by Kacey Musgraves

https://www.youtube.com/watch?v=m1VUNkukdHM

In this book I won't be telling you about how to drain your tanks, how to get your mail or how to get healthcare while on the road. You took care of those things before you hit the road.

Okay, maybe you're not on the road yet, so I will discuss these topics briefly in Chapter 14 when I talk about *Other Things You Need to Know.* One way or another you will learn all these basic things on your own about living in an RV.

I want to tell you about a lot of things you probably won't learn on your own—at least not the easy way, and I don't want you learning things about the RV lifestyle the hard way. If you wanted to learn everything the hard way, you wouldn't have bought this book.

Bottom line—what I wish I had known 7 years ago: The main purpose of this book is to tell you about the unusual things I've learned in seven years on the road that I wish I had known before I hit the road. Some things are funny, some helpful, some scary, some resulting from stupid mistakes, and some that don't fit into any category.

Chapter 1

You Have to Have a Dream

"You only live once, but if you do it right, once is enough."

~ Mae West

Do you have a dream of how you want to live your life and what you want to do?

By having a dream, I don't mean a dream such as, "I want to retire and not have to go to work," kind of dream. And I'm not talking about a daydream kind of dream.

I'm talking about what some people would call an unreal, crazy kind of dream—a dream that breathes new life into the dull routine of your day.

Imagine what it would be like to live anywhere you wanted to and be able to travel when and where you wanted to.

Hold that picture and thought in your mind and then compare that to the way your life is now. I don't think you want to continue to live in the same place, doing the same thing every day that you're doing now. If you did, you wouldn't be reading this book.

Which way would you be happier—your present lifestyle or living in an RV? You can't decide until you start dreaming and picturing yourself living the RVing lifestyle.

Nothing will happen until you start dreaming

When we were kids, we were always dreaming and playing make-believe. As we got older, dreaming was frowned on. Daydreaming was considered to be goofing off.

Forget about the stigma that sometimes goes with dreaming and start dreaming right now for real.

And if your dreams don't scare you, maybe they're not big enough

A lot of people think of a dream as wishful thinking. For example, they dream of winning the lottery.

But that kind of dream won't cut it. If you're going to make your dream of living in an RV a reality, your dream must be more than wishful thinking. It must be a burning desire.

It must be something you're going to make happen come hell or high water, as the saying goes.

That's the kind of dream you need if you're ever going to start living the full-time RVing lifestyle.

That's the way Becky Schade described the kind of dream you need in her book, *The Little Guide to Dreaming Big*. If you need help formulating your dream, here's a link to Becky's book:

https://www.amazon.com/dp/B01HREJMZK

Brittany and Eric at http://rvwanderlust.com/ put it this way:

"We chose the RV lifestyle not to escape life, but so that life doesn't escape us."

It's something to think about.

Now it's time for you to start dreaming about your RV lifestyle. Get busy dreaming and keep reading.

Have a dream, go for it, and make it happen.

Bottom line—what I wish I had known 7 years ago: I wish I had known seven years ago that having a dream is the most important thing when it comes to making the decision to live the RVing lifestyle.

Chapter 2

Cost of RVing

"Now is no time to think of what you do not have. Think of what you can do with what there is."

~ Ernest Hemingway

To paraphrase that quote, you could say that when you're thinking about retiring, or quitting your job and hitting the road, rather than think about how much money (or income) you will need, look at it from the opposite direction.

Look at the money (or income) you will have and decide what kind of life you can live with that money. RV living is as simple as that. You can live on way less than $1,000 a month and plenty of RVers are doing just that (I'll give you examples later in this chapter).

Even though you can RV on less than $1,000 a month, having a little more money available gives you a lot more freedom. There are plenty of ways to make more than $1,000 a month and those options are explained in Chapter 15.

Digging deeper into the cost of RVing

I could sum up this chapter about how much it costs to live full time in an RV by saying, "It depends," but you didn't come to this chapter to read, "It depends." You want a number.

Answering the question of how much it costs to live full time in an RV is like answering the question about how much it costs to live in a house—and it really does depend. It depends on the size of the house, the location, the condition of the house and the list goes on and on.

The same is true for living in an RV. I know you still want a number, so I'll stop rambling and give a number and a range of numbers.

The RVers I know spend between $1,000 and $4,000 a month to live in their RVs. Probably $2,000 to $3,000 a month would be about typical. I know some RVers who spend even less than $1,000 a month and some who spend more than $4,000 a month.

It will cost you about the same as what you're spending to live in a house or apartment, maybe a little less. Of course, it can be a lot less if you make some changes in how you live and how you spend your money.

RVers have a secret weapon for keeping costs down

One of the big advantages of living in an RV is that you have a lot of control over how much you spend each month. When you're living in a house, condo, or apartment, most of your expenses are pretty much fixed, and there's not much you can do to change them.

You can't cut your rent (or mortgage payment) back for a month or so when you're living in a house, condo or apartment.

But when you're living in an RV you can boondock for a month or so and eliminate campground fees. If you stay in one place, you're not spending any money on gas. If you're relying on solar power, you're not spending any money on electricity.

Except for food, insurance, and medical expenses, your costs to live in an RV could be almost zero. This is assuming that you're out of debt and not making payments on credit cards or student loans or having to make car, truck or RV payments.

If you're making payments on previous debt, that's not really part of your cost of living. That's paying for living you've already done but didn't pay for at the time.

Examples of RVing on $1,000 a month

The idea of RVing on $1,000 a month or less sounds nice, but are people really doing it? Since seeing is believing, I have provided links below to a few short YouTube videos showing RVers who are doing it.

Youtube.com/watch?v=fvP2XHMDdE4&t=9s — In this video Kyle and Olivia talk about how much they spend living full time in their RV. They go a little over the $1,000 a month number and spend about $1,300 a month, but that includes making payments on some credit card debt and paying off a student loan. So, their actual cost to live in their RV is about $1,000 a month.

Youtube.com/watch?v=XL60tPbY2YE — Here is a link to Robin's video where she discusses her budget and explains how she lives on a little less than $1,300 a month. She also shows you where she could get her living expenses down to less than $1,000 a month. For example, she spends $400 on food for one person. She could cut some out of that for sure. I would assume that she is eating out a lot.

Youtube.com/watch?v=sKRY6dR7Ae4&t=202s — Eric shows how he lives full time in his Class C motorhome and spends $655 a month, and that includes $100 a month on his cat. Is he feeding that cat caviar? He doesn't show anything in the budget for maintenance, but he can add $100 or so for maintenance and still be well under $1,000 a month.

Youtube.com/watch?v=VduibSuyHA4 — Bill goes over five years of his expenses, and he spent a little over $1,000 a month, but as you can see, he spent a lot of money on traveling and other things that you wouldn't buy if you were on a tight budget.

Youtube.com/watch?v=g_OmZzZD4rg — In this video Sam breaks down his monthly costs and shows how he spends $1,650 a month, but he spends $330 for gas and $450 for campground fees. He could travel less and boondock more and get his expenses below the $1,000 a month level.

As you can see, some of the people in these videos are spending more than $1,000 a month, but I think you can see how it would be easy for them to get their expenses down to $1,000 a month.

Having this option is like having a special reserve savings account. It's an option that's there any time you need it. For example, if you have a major repair bill and have to dig into your emergency fund to pay for the repair, you can go into boondocking mode for a month or two and build your emergency fund back up.

Just because it's possible to live on less than $1,000 a month that doesn't mean you should do it all the time. Just knowing that you can do it for a while if you needed to—because of the loss of one of your sources of income or because of needing to build your emergency fund back up—gives you a lot of security.

Bottom line—what I wish I had known 7 years ago: When I started RVing, I didn't realize how easy it would be to drop my living expenses to almost zero for a month (or two or three) by boondocking, not traveling, and just not spending any money (no eating out, and not buying stuff, etc.).

Having this option can take a lot of stress off you. It's an option I wish I had known about when I started RVing. It would have eliminated a lot of stress.

Chapter 3

Buying the Perfect RV

"Just living is not enough. One must have sunshine, freedom, and a little flower."

~ Hans Christian Anderson

Whether your idea of RVing and camping is having a pup tent and a kayak or a large Class A motorhome, you'll find people who share your enthusiasm for that style of camping.

They're both considered RVing or camping and each one is the perfect choice—for that person.

RVs sell for prices that range from one thousand dollars to over one million dollars. Some sell for up to two or three million dollars, but we won't spend time talking about those. If you could afford one of those, you wouldn't be reading this book. But they are fun to walk through when you're attending RV shows.

Let's get back down to Earth. All our lives we've wanted bigger, fancier, and better things.

It's easy for that habit to carry over into how we go about selecting an RV. I bought a 34-foot Class A motorhome, which is way bigger than I need just for me. I don't even have a dog, so for sure, I don't need an RV this big.

If I were going to be boondocking in some remote places, it would really be too big, but since I don't boondock in places that are hard to get to, it's not a big deal. I do enjoy the space this big RV gives me, so I'm not going to get rid of the motorhome I have now and get another one anytime soon. I've made a lot of modifications to it and added a lot of gadgets to it, and I'm happy with it. It's like one of the family now.

Which type of RV is best for full-time living?

Everyone who is considering the RV lifestyle spends a lot of time stressing out over what type of RV they should buy. There are motorhomes, fifth wheels, travel trailers, and then, when it comes to motorhomes, there are Class A, Class B, Class C, and converted vans, converted buses, and the list goes on and on.

And to make the choice even harder, all these different types of RVs come in a wide variety of different lengths.

It's only natural that if it's going to be your home, you want to make the right choice. In other words, you want to pick the perfect RV for you and for your lifestyle, but that's impossible.

The problem is there's no one type of RV that's perfect for the RVing lifestyle. And even if there were an RV that was perfect for you, you wouldn't know how to find it or even be able to recognize it if you did find it. Here's why:

- You don't know much about RVs or what kind you would be happy with.
- You don't know much about how or where you'll be traveling.
- And even if you did know all of this, more than likely, your wants will change after you start RVing.

Two years ago, a friend of mine sold his house and decided to live and travel full time in an RV. The one thing he was sure about was that he didn't want to do any boondocking. He wanted to always be in an RV park with full hookups (water, electric, and sewer).

Since he was so sure that this was what he wanted to do, he bought a camper that didn't have holding tanks.

I'm sure you're already ahead of me, but he soon decided that he loved boondocking. That's all he wants to do. So now he has bought another camper with solar, and, of course, holding tanks.

Leave your check book at home (so you can't be talked into buying something) and visit some RV dealers. Go inside several RVs (Class, A, B, C, fifth wheel, campers, etc.). Look at the floor plan, sit on the couch, sit on the john, and stretch out across the bed. In other words, picture yourself living in that RV. Be sure to check out the different sizes of each type of RV.

After you have an idea of the basic type of RV you think you want (Class A motorhome, Class B, camper, etc.), your next step is to do your research and find out what the fair market value is of the type of RV you think you want. Keep the fact in mind that it probably won't be the RV you will have or want in a year or two regardless of how perfect you think it seems now.

Of course, when you find out what the fair market value is of the RV you want, keep in mind that the fair market value is not the price you want to pay. You want to buy an RV for less than it's worth. But you can't do that until you do enough research to know what a certain type of RV is worth.

As my father always told me, you make your money when you buy something—not when you sell it. You can expect to sell it for about what it's worth. Your goal is to buy it for less than it's worth.

How do you find out the true market value of an RV?

You can't recognize a bargain when you find it if you don't know the true market value of the type of RV you're looking for. So, after you have an idea of what type of RV you're looking for, you need to find out what the fair market value of that RV is.

Here are some sources that can give you that information:

First, don't go by the asking price or sticker price of the used RVs on dealers' lots. Many times, they will drop the asking price in half when you get down to some serious negotiating.

Below is a link to a website that shows what RVs have recently sold for.

Pplmotorhomes.com/sold/soldmenu.htm

This site tells you what RVs have recently sold for. The people at PPL Motorhomes sell about 4,000 motorhomes a year, and they show you what each one actually sold for.

They also always have a huge inventory of used RVs for sale. Most of them are on consignment.

Another way to see what RVs are selling for is to check eBay and look at RVs that sold. Don't pay any attention to the asking prices. The sold price is the only price that matters.

Selecting the right RV

There are a lot of videos with advice about which type of RV is best for full-time living. Obviously, there's no one right type of RV. You will find people enjoying RVing full time in every type of RV you can imagine.

And if you ask them, most of them will tell you that they love their RV. In other words, you can't get an unbiased opinion of which type of RV is the best by asking RV owners.

Some people are surprised to find out that after a year or two many people decide a different RV would fit their needs better. Surprisingly, most people want a smaller RV. I don't think I know of anyone who wanted a larger RV.

If you follow Becky Schade's blog at InstellerOrchard.com, you will learn that after five years in a 17-foot Casita camper she sold it and bought a smaller camper.

My opinion

Buy an RV that you can afford to pay cash for if possible. Don't worry about finding the perfect RV. Within a year or two you'll want to sell it and get a different one. I know I've said that before, but I want it to sink in. It's important that you believe this.

In a nutshell, for full-time RV living, I would recommend going with an RV like the one I have. (Of course, most other RVers will tell you that too—go with an RV like the one they have.)

In other words, a used (it can be very used) Class A with two slides (unless you plan on doing a lot of boondocking in rough terrain or you're going to be a solo RVer). Class A motorhomes don't have a lot of ground clearance, so there are a lot of boondocking places that you can't get to in a Class A RV. Keep this in mind.

One of the main advantages of a Class A is that it has a lot of storage space in what is called the basement, which is the storage bins under the RV. (I guess that's why that space is called the basement.) Other classes of motorhomes and campers don't have nearly as much storage space. Fifth wheel RVs do have more storage than the other RVs but not as much as a Class A.

A Class A is not the right choice for everyone and may not be the right choice for you. Do your research and legwork.

A lot of people like campers (or travel trailers as they are also called). They have better ground clearance and can get into more boondocking places than a Class A or even a Class C motorhome. If you're traveling solo, you could look at Class C RVs or maybe even a van. Class B RVs are small, easy to drive, and get good gas mileage. They are very popular, and that makes them expensive.

If you're on a tight budget and plan to live in your RV full time, I wouldn't recommend a Class B, but I have a lot of friends who have them and love them. As Shakespeare said, "To each his own."

There's no right way to RV, and for sure there's no RV that's right for everyone or for every type of RVing.

Some people recommend going with a diesel engine. Diesels have a more power, but they're more expensive to buy and more expensive to maintain. With my gas engine, I have to go slow up mountains, but I'm not in that big of a hurry. If I were going to be traveling a lot in the Rockies, I might wish I had the power of a diesel engine.

There are advantages and disadvantages to the other types of RVs. The Class C motorhomes are easier to drive and get a little better gas mileage than a Class A, but there is not much storage. If you're going to live in your RV full time, you'll appreciate the extra storage space that a Class A RV has.

A lot of people love the Class B RVs and vans, and they would work well for one person and especially if you were going to be traveling a lot or doing a lot of boondocking.

Fifth wheel RVs have more room. If you have kids, this could come in handy. You could have a bedroom up front and another bedroom or bunk beds in the back. The bedrooms are separated by the kitchen and living area. They are easier to tow than a camper/trailer.

A lot of people love camper/trailers. Since they started RVing four years ago, Nathan and Marissa have had four different RVs (Class A, fifth-wheel, and two campers). Now they have an Airstream camper and love it. They say it's just right for their family of three and the way they travel and camp. They like to boondock a lot in remote areas. Check out their YouTube channel at Less Junk-More Journey. (Update: In the spring of 2019, they are expecting an addition to their family of three, so they may sell their Airstream and get a larger RV in a year or so.)

The only thing that really matters when selecting your first RV is to buy one you can afford and buy one that you can sell in a year or so and at least get your money back and maybe even make a profit on.

The real answer is to listen to Lidia's advice on her YouTube channel *SimpleRVing. She says, "Listen to your soul. Simplify and go."*

Is it possible to get a low-cost RV that's functional?

I know a lot of people who have hit the road in RVs that they paid $5,000 to $10,000 for and sometimes even less.

Here's an example of someone spending even less. Brett bought a 1985 Coachman Class C motorhome recently for $800 and hit the road. He drove it 1,000 miles on his first trip, and everything worked fine. He has been living in it now for over a year, and everything is still working.

Below is a link to a video of him describing his $800 motorhome.

Youtube.com/watch?v=T_EoN9AkRek

Below are two links to Class A motorhomes that were purchased for $500 each.

Youtube.com/watch?v=n6_opku2Iik&t=28s

Youtube.com/watch?v=ITR6EmsW7ks

When you're buying a used RV (whether you're paying $1,000 or $100,000), be sure to check the date code on the tires. Don't look at the tread on the tires like you would if you were buying a used car.

It's okay to buy an RV when the tires are almost aged out, but make sure you know this and plan to spend $2,500 to $3,000 or so for tires soon after you buy the RV. In other words, factor that cost into the price you're paying and see if you still like the deal.

RV tires don't wear out, they age out. Ozone and UV light cause a tire to deteriorate. (It's called dry rot.) RV tires are good for five to seven years. After that tires will start to crack and become dangerous to drive on.

To tell the age of the tires on the RV you're looking at, look for the 4-digit date code on the tires (sometimes it's on the inside and you have to crawl under the RV to see it). It's the last four digits in the series of number and letters that start with "DOT" as shown in the photo below.

The first two digits are the week and the second two are the year the tire was manufactured. The tire in the photo was made in the third week of 2013.

This tire was manufactured in the third week of 2013

Note: I've included this picture and description of how to determine the age of RV tires in most of my other RVing books. If you've read some of my other books, I'm sorry for the repetition, but this fact is so important (and it's not covered in a lot of other books about RVing) that I want to make sure all RV owners know this information.

The one thing you should never believe

The one thing RV sellers (both dealers and individuals) will tell you that you should never believe without checking for yourself is that the tires are good. Sometimes they will even point out how much tread is left on the tires. **RV tires don't wear out they age out.** It's not that everyone selling an RV is dishonest. Some people just don't know. Don't take anyone's word about tires. Check for yourself—even if you have to crawl under the RV to find the date code.

Having a tire blow out is one of the most common things that cause RV wrecks. Some of these wrecks are fatal. I hate to say it, but I've had RV salesmen tell me how good the tires on an RV are by pointing out how much tread is left on the tires. Don't fall for this. Check the date code for yourself. Know what you're buying.

You must negotiate when buying an RV

Some people don't like to negotiate and some people who do like to negotiate do it all wrong. In other words, they're not very good at it, and some people think they're good negotiators when they're not, and they get taken to the cleaners.

Negotiating doesn't have to be a hassle or an unpleasant experience. Just use one or more of the seven statements below and watch the asking price start to decrease in a hurry. If you use these statements, negotiating can be a fun experience.

Here are my seven all-time favorite negotiating phrases for people who don't like to negotiate

1. ALWAYS, ALWAYS flinch at the first price or proposal.
2. Next, when you get the lower price offer, you should say, "You've got to do better than that."
3. If you make a counter offer, always ask for a much lower price than you expect to get.
4. Never offer to split the difference. The other party is almost always willing to do that, so try to get a slightly better deal than that.
5. Use two powerful negotiating techniques in one sentence. The two techniques are "Absent higher authority" and "If I could, would you?" We've all experienced the "Absent higher authority" technique. For example, "Our insurance regulations won't let you go back in the shop," or "The loan committee wouldn't go along with those

terms." Here's how to use the technique in your favor for once. When you're down to the final negotiations, you can say, "If I could get my (financial adviser, spouse or some absent higher authority) to go along with this, would you replace the two front tires?"

6. Nibble for more at the end. You can usually get a little bit more even after you have basically agreed on everything. You can say, "You ARE going to have the carpets professionally cleaned (or you are going to replace the windshield wiper blades), aren't you?"
7. When you're getting close to the end of the negotiations and everything is just about nailed down, say, "I'm getting nervous about this," and then SHUT UP. A lot of times this technique will get you one more concession. This technique works well when a woman says it because men tend to believe women change their minds sometimes for no logical reason. (I wonder why men think that.)

If you follow the information in this chapter, you can end up with an RV that's right for you and for thousands of dollars less than you would spend if you went the conventional route of buying an RV.

After a year on the road you will want a different RV

Finding and buying your first RV is a simple process since you only have one criterion. That one criterion is to find an RV that you can sell in a year or so for at least what you paid for it and hopefully even more. In other words, one you can sell in a year or so and make a profit on it.

The reason is simple, over half of the people I know who live in an RV sell their first one within a year or two and get a different one. And even more people wish they could, but they bought a new RV and they would lose their shirt if they sold their new RV after only having it for a year or so.

More information about how to buy a motorhome

Buying a Used Motorhome – How to get the most for your money and not get burned by Bill Myers.

Don't even think about buying a motorhome without reading this book. The information in this book saved me thousands of dollars. And, more importantly, it helped me pick the right motorhome for my needs and budget.

The book is about buying a used motorhome, but a lot of the information would also be useful and helpful if you were considering buying a travel trailer or fifth wheel camper. You can find the book on Amazon at this link:

Amazon.com/dp/B007OV4TBY

Summary of how to find and buy your first RV

The simple answer is to do enough soul searching and research to decide what type of RV you think you want. Then do research to determine what a fair price would be for the RV you want, and then the most important thing is to do your research to find that RV at a price that is less than a fair price. You want a bargain. Keep looking until you find one.

One final point: Before you buy any RV, spend the $200 to $500 (depending on the level of inspection you want) to have it inspected. When you agree on a price, always include in your offer the words, "Subject to it passing my RV mechanic's inspection, and everything being as represented."

Even after you have already settled on the price, you can usually negotiate the price down enough to more than cover the inspection cost by bringing up the things the inspector found that you didn't know when you agreed on the price.

You can find certified RV inspectors in your area at **nrvia.org/locate**. Another option is to get a local RV mechanic to do the inspection for you.

Do your research to determine what type of RV will be best for you. Next look at your budget and the cash you have available. Then use the methods described in this chapter to find the RV you're looking for and be sure to use some or all the negotiating techniques I've outlined to get an even better deal.

My advice is to buy a used RV at a price that will allow you to sell it in a year or two and at least get your money back and hopefully even make a profit. It can be done if you do your homework and learn how to negotiate. If you clean it up, wax the RV, and fix a few things, that will increase the value of it also.

The worst thing you can do is buy a new RV and then be upside down on it in a year or two. You don't want to be in a situation where you owe more on your RV than you can sell it for. And that's the situation you will almost surely be in if you buy a new RV.

It doesn't matter whether you buy a Class A, a travel trailer, a Class C, or a fifth wheel, no choice will be wrong if you buy an RV that you can sell within a year or so and get your money back.

Well, if you bought a Class B and you have three kids and two dogs, you might soon find out that you made a wrong choice, but since you bought your RV at a good price and can sell it without losing money, even that situation could have a happy ending.

Yes, spend some time looking at RVs and give it your best shot at deciding what type of RV would be best for you, but in the end, just get one (at a good price) and go.

Almost every RVer I know (including me) spent a lot of time trying to decide which RV would be the best for them (and in most cases they didn't get the right one after all).

Bottom line—what I wish I had known 7 years ago: I wish I known that deciding what kind of RV would be best for me was not as important as I thought it was, and I shouldn't have fretted over the decision so much. I wish someone had told me to just buy a used RV (at a bargain price) and hit the road.

I wish I had known the simple fact that the best RV for me was one that I could buy at a great price. By a great price I mean buy it at less than it was worth.

Chapter 4

Emotions to Deal With

"All emotion is involuntary when genuine."

~ Mark Twain

As Mark Twain said, we don't have any control over the emotions we feel. They are involuntary.

We do have control over how we deal with our emotions. Emotions are easier to deal with when we see them coming. It's harder to deal with an emotion you didn't expect.

Pointing out the emotions you're likely to experience is what this chapter is about.

When it all hits you at one time

When you leave your job, your home, your community, and your friends all at one time, that will drum up a lot of emotions. It will probably cause a lot more emotions than you expected, and they won't all come to light at once.

Stress and emotions will pop up from time to time long after you think you've dealt with everything. Be prepared for those feelings.

To make things even harder, initially, you probably won't have a support group around you. None of your close friends have ever done anything like what you're about to do.

Yeah, there are a lot of YouTube videos posted by people that you may feel like you know because you've watched so many of their videos, but they are not part of your support group, at least not yet.

Some of your friends might be saying, "Yeah, go for it," but, truthfully, they don't know anything about the RVing lifestyle. And they sure don't know anything about the emotions you will be dealing with. My guess is that most of your friends don't think you should do it (even if they don't say so directly).

You can analyze all the numbers and the financial part of RVing, but you can't put a number on the emotional part.

This is the biggest unknown and probably the scariest part of setting out on living the RV lifestyle.

Here are some of the emotional questions that will haunt you

- Will my family and friends think I've lost my mind? (Some may think you're crazy—others will be sure.)
- Will I get lonely?
- Am I being realistic?
- Will I run out of money?
- Is this a mistake?
- What if my RV breaks down and leaves me stranded?
- What if I get sick?
- Will living 24/7 in a cramped space with my spouse and family drive me crazy?
- If I'm RVing solo, how will I handle living 24/7 by myself—especially if I'm boondocking and not around other people?
- Can I deal with being away from family and friends?

Don't let the naysayers discourage you from living your dream. Don't take advice about RVing from someone who has never done it.

As my grandmother used to tell me, ***"People are down on what they're not up on."*** In other words, they're against things they don't know anything about. You'll experience that reaction throughout the planning phase of your adventure. Be prepared for it.

The song, "Don't Worry. Be Happy" was written by Bob McFerrin and made popular by Bob Marley. It's a beautiful song with some wonderful advice. No wonder it's been watched over 114 million times on YouTube. I'm sure you've heard the song, but if you want to hear it again, here's a link to it.

https://www.youtube.com/watch?v=L3HQMbQAWRc

How true the words of the song are, so don't worry. Just be happy.

Take a minute and listen to the song. You'll be glad you did.

I wrote a book last year titled *RVing Less Hassle—More Joy*. The subtitle of the book is *Secrets of Having More Fun with Your RV—Even on a Limited Budget.*

You don't need this book yet. You're still deciding if you want to live the RVing lifestyle and if so, how to go about it.

Later, after you get on the road, you might find that book interesting and helpful. But for now, stick to your project of getting the information you need to make your decision about whether the full-time RVing lifestyle is right for you, and how to go about it.

Telling your family and friends

Some people stress about how to announce their plans to their family and friends. The idea of doing this is sometimes more stressful than actually doing it.

Here's how to keep it from being stressful. Just don't discuss your thoughts and plans with anyone (except your spouse) until you have done your homework, have answers to most of your questions, and have pretty well made up your mind that living full time in an RV is what you're going to do.

Then start by only announcing it to one or two close friends you think will support your decision. Get their support under your belt before you start telling the world.

When you do announce it to everyone, expect to hear a lot of people tell you why it won't work and how crazy and stupid you are for even considering it. Of course, they probably won't use those exact words, but that's the message that will come across to you (and believe me, in many cases, that's what they will be thinking).

You'll hear comments like this

- You can't be serious.
- Have you thought this through?
- I would never do that.
- What you're talking about is not realistic.
- There's no way you can make a living on the road.

You might even get a few comments like the following, but probably not many.

- I would love to do that.
- I'm so happy for you.
- You are so brave.
- That's what I want to do someday.

Make sure your mind is made up that you're going to live full time in an RV before you mention it to your family and friends.

Then remember that you're telling them as a courtesy. You're not asking for their opinions, blessings or approvals. The good news is that you don't have to worry about what anyone thinks or says. It's your life and you're going to live it the way you want to.

When you've done your homework, have the answers and solutions to all your questions and concerns, no one can burst your bubble. At this point, it's good to remember what Steve Jobs said.

"Don't let the noise of others' opinions drown out your own inter voice. And most important, have the courage to follow your heart and intuition."

~ Steve Jobs

Anytime things change, there will be emotions to deal with, and, believe me, transitioning into living the full-time RVing life is a big change. Expect to deal with a lot of emotions. The emotions won't hit you all at once. About the time you think you have adjusted to everything more emotions will hit you.

Emotions are stressful. Expect that, but don't let your emotions keep you from living your dream. Remember what Helen Keller said in the quote below:

"Life is either a great adventure or nothing at all."

~ Helen Keller

When you're making this big of a change in your life, there will be a lot of emotions to deal with.

One of the biggest emotions you'll have to deal with is the constant gnawing feeling of "What if."

RVing emotions fall into one of two categories

The two categories are—emotions before you hit the road and emotions after you get on the road.

Here are some of the emotions you will be dealing with before you hit the road:

- Selling your house or moving out of your apartment
- Getting rid of your stuff
- Dealing with reactions and comments from family and friends
- Going over and over the numbers and deciding if you can really do it
- Dealing with all of the unknowns
- The constant "what if" questions in your head

If you have a dream of living full time in an RV and you're not doing it yet, my guess is that fear is holding you back. It's not the money (maybe it's the fear of running out of money).

The idea of taking a risk conjures up feelings of fear. It's a normal and natural reaction. Fear helps keep us safe, but sometimes it's easy to let fear have more control over our actions than is warranted.

One of the best ways to overcome fear is to arm yourself with knowledge and information. The more you know about a situation the less fear there will be in the decision to go forward.

I think that's what you're doing by reading this book. You're getting the information you need to make an informed decision and implement it.

Don't be afraid that something will go wrong

Accept the fact that for sure something will go wrong, and then something else will go wrong. That's the RVing lifestyle. If you can't handle that, this life is not for you.

Fear shows up in many forms

There's the fear of getting hurt like why we didn't want to jump off the high diving board when we were kids. That's not the fear you're dealing with here. You don't really think you might get hurt if you start living the RVing lifestyle.

Here are some of the fears you're probably concerned about (even though you may not want to admit all of them).

- Fear that your friends will think you're being totally irresponsible
- Fear that you'll run out of money
- Fear that you'll blow what money you have and have to come home and try to find a job and a place to live
- Fear that you won't like the lifestyle and then have to admit that you were wrong
- Fear of embarrassment when things don't work out

The risk of change

Accept the fact that making a change involves taking a risk.

One final thought: You can't plan everything regardless of how much time you take getting everything ready for your RVing adventure. When I was in engineering school, almost all my time was spent learning how to design things. But when I started working as an engineer, I found out that I spent a lot more time testing designs than I ever spent doing the actual designs. I found out that's the way engineering works. In school, I don't remember ever testing anything.

You've planned everything. Your testing will start when you hit the road.

You can't plan for everything. Well, you can. It's called an emergency fund.

There may be valid reasons why you can't live full time in an RV right now (aging parents you need to take care of, a business or house you need to sell, etc.), but don't let fear be one of the reasons you don't hit the road. Fear is useful to help you make sure you've looked at all the factors involved, but it shouldn't be a reason not to take the plunge.

Bottom line—what I wish I had known 7 years ago: Being an engineer, I looked at everything from a logical standpoint. I cranked and tweaked the numbers, and everything said, "Go."

What I wish I had known was that, regardless of how much analyzing you have done, when you leave your job, your home, your community, and your friends all at one time, it will drum up a lot of emotions. You will feel a lot more emotions than you expected, and they won't all come to light at once.

I wish I had known that stress and emotions will pop up from time to time long after you think you've dealt with everything. Be prepared for those feelings (I wasn't).

Chapter 5

Making the Decision

"Live your life by a compass not a clock."

~ Stephen Covey

Are you still undecided about RVing? My guess is that you've already been indoctrinated somewhat about how wonderful the RVing lifestyle is.

It is wonderful, at least, a lot of people say it is, but that's not the whole story.

We all fret over making big decisions. We can never have all the facts. There will always be more "What if" concerns. The more unknowns, the harder the decision is to make.

Look at it this way, you're probably not completely happy with the life you're living now, or you wouldn't be reading this book and you wouldn't seriously be considering making a big change in your life to start living full time in an RV.

With that fact in mind, realize that when you have your house sold or rented (or you move out of your apartment or condo) and you've gotten rid of most of your stuff, you are free as a bird to live whatever lifestyle you choose.

You may not have stopped to think about it, but your house is a burden—even if it's paid for. You may not realize it until it happens, but when you get rid of your house and most of your stuff, it will feel like a big load has been lifted from you. You will feel free to make decisions in a way you haven't felt in a long time—if ever.

If you try living the RVing lifestyle and decide that you don't like it, you probably don't want to go back to the life you're living now (which you're not happy with).

When you choose the RVing lifestyle, you're not locked into it. You can always sell your RV and get your money back (if you followed my previous advice about buying a used RV at a bargain price).

I love the RVing lifestyle and I have no intention of going back to a stick-and-brick house, condo or apartment. I do plan on going back to Costa Rica for a few months this spring. I'll probably spend a few months in a different country every year for a while.

I can rent a house or apartment in another country for $500 to $600 a month or I can pay $500 to $600 a month to stay in a campground. My cost of living is approximately the same whichever I do, so why not do both. I can cancel the liability and collision insurance on my motorhome and store it. The savings on the insurance more than cover the cost of storing the RV.

This freedom to travel and live in a different country from time to time is just one of the many advantages of the RV lifestyle that I love.

To make a decision you need facts

Here are some of the not so fun and glamorous facts about the RVing lifestyle that probably no one has told you about. I didn't know these things when I started RVing, but I don't think knowing these things would have changed my mind—but they might change your mind, so let's go over them.

Here are some of the things that are not so wonderful about RVing

- If you like to work on things, there is always something on an RV that needs to be fixed. If you don't like to work on things, there is still always something on an RV that needs to be fixed.
- There's no way around it. You can't take all your stuff with you. You must get rid of a LOT of things.
- Face it. There is not a lot of space in an RV. It's a totally different way to live.
- All RVs depreciate, and new ones depreciate fast.
- Medical care can be expensive if you're not old enough to be on Medicare and you travel and stay out of network a lot.
- For some people, constantly being away from friends and family (especially grandkids) can be a big problem. And for some people, it's a deal killer.
- For most people, when they become full-time RVers, they must learn to get by with less income. If you like to go shopping, buy a lot of new clothes, go out to eat a lot, and always have the latest gadgets, the RVing lifestyle might not be worth the sacrifices required to live the lifestyle.

A lot of people worry about the uncertainty of living the full-time RVing life. They worry about things such as:

- Will I like the lifestyle?
- Can I afford it?
- What if I don't like the lifestyle?
- Will my friends think I've lost my mind?
- And the list of worries goes on and on

Yes, there are some real reasons why some people can't live the RVing lifestyle right now, but for a lot of people, I think it comes down to not being able to make a decision and then make it happen.

You may be thinking, *But I've quit my job and sold my house. I can't go back. What if I don't like the RVing lifestyle?* Look at it this way. You already know you're unhappy with your job, and your present lifestyle, so why would you want to go back?

You shouldn't want your old job back. *Forbes, Fortune, Harvard Review,* and several major business magazines have said that you should change jobs and maybe even careers every four to five years.

There will always be unknowns. You will never have all the answers. Most of the full-time RVers I talk to say their only regret is that they didn't do it sooner.

It's true that the RVing lifestyle is not all rainbows, sunsets, and margaritas, but enough of it is that after living full time in my RV for seven years, I wouldn't want to go back to living in a stick-and-brick house, condo, or apartment. No way. (And I don't even like margaritas.)

Bottom line—what I wish I had known 7 years ago: Like everyone else considering living the RVing lifestyle, I spent a lot of time, effort, and frustration trying to make the decision. I wish I had realized the simple fact that I wanted to live a different life and if the RVing lifestyle turned out not to be what I wanted to do, it would be so easy to change my mind and live another lifestyle.

I kept thinking it was a major decision and it wasn't. I wish I had known that.

Chapter 6

Life on the Road

"I buy expensive suits. They just look cheap on me."

~ Warren Buffett

I've learned a lot about living the RVing lifestyle in the seven years I've been on the road. But I think I've learned more about myself.

I know what I like and what I don't like. One of the most important things I learned is to say, "No," to things I don't want to do. I copied this concept from Warren Buffett.

He has a lot of people vying for his time and presenting him with opportunities for him to consider. The way he handles all these demands (or, at least, requests) for his time is simple.

If it's not a "Hell, yes, let's do it," it's a "No."

My time is spent doing only things I want to do. If I were traveling with someone, I would be accommodating and do things we both enjoy doing, but that's not the case in my situation. That's one of the big advantages of solo RVing.

In the seven years I've been on the road living full time in my RV, I've heard a lot of people tell me what a wonderful life I'm living and how they wish they could live like I'm living.

Most of them could, but they're afraid to take a risk. They had rather stay with their comfortable but boring life than take a risk and do something different.

In the seven years I've been on the road, I've realized that whether someone is happy with the RVing lifestyle or unhappy. . .

It all comes down to attitude

It's like Tom Sawyer whitewashing the fence. Whether it's work or fun depends on your attitude.

Here are the four prevailing attitudes I've found you must have to enjoy "Life on the Road" as a full-time RVer:

1. Get rid of your stuff

Getting rid of all the things you don't need is so liberating. When you first start deciding what to get rid of, it's scary. You'll hear yourself saying, "I might need this sometime." You're right. You might, but probably not.

If you do need something that you got rid of, there are two options. You can probably get by without the item just fine. The second option is, because you're not out in the wilderness like Lewis and Clark, there is usually at least a trading post nearby that will have the item. And Amazon can deliver it to you in two days (one day if you're really in a hurry).

Most people make two mistakes when downsizing. The first mistake is that they take way too much stuff with them. The second mistake is that they put too much stuff in a storage unit.

You'll probably make both mistakes too. I know I did. Don't worry. In six months to a year, you can downsize again and get rid of most of the items you brought with you and most of the items in your storage shed that you're paying rent on. You might have to do this downsizing a few times to finally get rid of the junk you have accumulated.

It's a wonderful feeling when all that stuff is gone. It's liberating to be rid of it.

One of the things I found most rewarding about RVing full time was when I got rid of all my stuff. The storage bins under my Class A motorhome are called the basement area and it still fills up with junk just like a real basement. Every so often I have to clean out all the junk that accumulates.

2. Go with the flow

New RVers worry that something is going to go wrong. Experienced RVers accept the fact that something is going to go wrong and then something else is going to go wrong. Things are going to break; travel plans are going to change.

If there were no unknowns, there would be no adventure. Keep this idea in mind and go with the flow.

Carve your plans in Jell-O or carve them in sand. None of your plans should be carved in stone.

Stay flexible and see where the RVing life takes you. Some of my most enjoyable and memorable times were unplanned.

Until you learn to go with the flow, you'll find yourself dealing with a lot of stress. Stress and joy can't co-exist. Most (probably all) of your stress is self-imposed. There's no place you have to be, and there's no time you have to be there.

3. Go slow

Maybe being lazy and moving slow comes natural for some people, but most of us like to get things done and move on to the next thing. We've been rushing so long that we don't know how to do things any other way.

It takes time and practice before going slow feels natural. Sometimes I still feel guilty when I look back at what I've accomplished for the day and decide that I haven't really accomplished much of anything. After seven years I'm beginning to get good at having a day where I don't accomplish anything and not feeling guilty about it.

A lot of RVers start out with plans to visit all the national parks, and they take off in a whirlwind. That takes the joy out of the experience. The national parks are not going anywhere. They'll be there next year and the year after.

The real joy of the RVing life can only be experienced when you slow down. I only drive a few thousand miles a year. I stay in most areas for at least a month, and most of the time for even longer periods of time. I enjoy getting to experience the area and know the people.

Most RVers when they start out are like a whirlwind. They are not relaxing, and they are also blowing through their money. The quicker you learn that you can't keep up that pace the better. Even if you could keep the pace up, it's not an enjoyable way to live. If that's the way you are going to live, you might as well go back to the hectic way of life you left.

Almost every full-time RVer will tell you to slow down, but most RVers (including me) must learn this for themselves. Hopefully, you can realize the joy of slowing down within a month or two, but some RVers take up to a year before they learn to slow down.

4. Get to know and enjoy the new people you meet

Motivational speaker Charlie "Tremendous" Jones put it this way:

"You will be the same person in five years as you are today except for the people you meet and the books you read."

When you're a full-time RVer, you'll have plenty of time to read books, and you'll also meet a lot of interesting people—both fellow RVers and the locals. Take the time to get to know them.

The people you meet are movers and shakers. They are people who make decisions, take risks, and make things happen. You will find them to be a lot more interesting than the people you knew back home.

You will find that they have done some interesting things. For example, I met an RVer recently who used to fly Air Force One. As you might guess, he had a lot of interesting stories to tell.

I could write a whole chapter about the interesting people I've met during the seven years I've been on the road. As you might guess, the people who have done interesting things in their life are the ones who took a risk and are living full time in their RVs.

If you want to have a fun and interesting life, get busy reading books and meeting other RVers. You will find that RVers are some of the friendliest and most interesting people on the planet.

RVers are easy to meet and you'll find that they love to talk to you. Maybe it's because when they're stuck in their RV all day with nobody to talk to except their spouse, they would welcome a chance to talk to somebody else. Just a thought.

You have to spend time to really get to know people. I had known the Air Force One pilot for over a month before we got around to talking about what he used to do before he retired.

By the way, not all interesting people are retired. Some of the young RVers I meet are extremely interesting.

Don't restrict yourself to just meeting fellow RVers. Get to know some of the locals everywhere you go. You'll find their stories, ideas, and insights intriguing.

I have a writing friend and she says that anytime she needs a new character for one of her novels, she just goes to a local watering hole or goes to the city park and sits on a park bench and starts talking to the people she meets. Sometimes they are just the character she needs and sometimes they start talking about somebody in the town and that person is the character she is looking for.

Of course, she doesn't use their real names, and she doesn't tell them she is going to use them as a character in one of her books. She said, "You can't make up characters like the real people I meet or learn about when I'm traveling."

One other thing I wish I had known seven years ago, when I was getting ready to hit the road and start RVing full time was how easy the transition was going to be. I assumed that it would be a difficult transition, getting rid of most of my stuff, leaving family and friends, and adjusting to all the unknowns.

The truth is that it was almost a non-issue. There was nothing to the transition. There was so much fun and excitement that I totally forgot about all the things I worried about when I was making my plans to hit the road.

Bottom line—what I wish I had known 7 years ago: I did know that I needed to get rid of a lot of stuff, but I didn't know or even think about the concepts of going slow, going with the flow, or the joys of getting to know the interesting people I would meet.

If someone had explained these concepts to me seven years ago (and if I had listened to them), my early days of RVing would have been so much more interesting, enjoyable, and less stressful.

Chapter 7

Solo RVing

"The man who goes alone can start today; but he who travels with another must wait till that other is ready."

~ Henry David Thoreau

There are a lot of advantages to RVing solo. I have been RVing solo for seven years. I don't even have a dog. It's just me and my motorhome. I love the lifestyle, and I like the idea of traveling alone.

Solo RVing is exciting, challenging, and full of amazing experiences. One of the things I like about solo RVing is that I can change my mind at any crossroads.

The decisions are mine to make, and the consequences are mine to bear.

Don't worry

It's easy to say, "Don't worry," but I'm sure you would like to have some information and facts to keep you from worrying. Let me fill in some blanks.

If you're concerned about traveling solo, my simple answer is don't be. I meet a lot, and I do mean a lot, of solo RVers. (Surprisingly, I see more women solo RVers than men.)

Contrary to what I expected, I've never met a solo RVer who has ever experienced any loneliness, safety, or security concerns while traveling as a solo RVer.

I meet a lot of solo RVers who thought they might be lonely, but they soon realized that no one is lonely when they're RVing (unless they want some alone time).

Solo RVing is safe

One of the main reasons it's so safe is that there's no riff-raff in RV parks or in the boondocking areas where RVers camp.

Think about it; if a person wanted to steal something, the pickings are not very good inside an RV. What would they steal? There's nothing in an RV that someone could walk off with and sell except maybe a computer. Take an old computer into a pawn shop and see what they will offer you for it.

I don't think I have locked my motorhome in over a year. (Maybe I should start now since I've told the world that my motorhome is sitting there unlocked.)

Even if someone tried to break into your RV, you could blow your horn or open the window and scream. That would quickly bring more help and bring it faster than if you called 911 while living in a traditional house or apartment.

In other words, with a little common sense and reasonable precautions, you're safer in an RV than you would be in most houses or apartments.

Solo RVing groups

You'll find solo RVers everywhere. I'm sitting in my motorhome in a campground in Florida right now and when I look out the windshield, I see two RVs occupied by solo women RVers. There are more solo RVers in other parts of the park.

I met two solo RVers in a restaurant last night. One had been RVing for three months and the other one for only a week.

If you're planning on being a solo RVer, you will find plenty of company. If you want to connect with even more solo RVers than just the ones you run into, here are some organizations that are focused on solo RVers.

- **RVingWomen.org**
- **LonersOnWheels.com**
- **RVSingles.org**

These are not dating or matchmaking sites, just groups of solo RVers with a common interest in the RVing lifestyle.

Solo RVing videos

One way to quickly get a feel for how solo RVers feel about their lifestyle is to watch a few short videos of them talking about their life and experiences.

There are hundreds of solo RVer videos on YouTube. Below are six of my favorites:

Note: If you watch these six short videos where solo RVers tell you about their lives and you don't fall in love with the idea of solo RVing, then one thing is for sure—solo RVing is not for you.

Becky Schade:

Youtube.com/watch?v=ebbo800_Rg0&t=2s

Alex: **Youtube.com/watch?v=3nMBNAlHQMo&t=7s**

Pippi Peterson: **Youtube.com/watch?v=X1EIdQN5rq0**

Lidia: **Youtube.com/watch?v=-TS0zDISyRU**

Lidia: **Youtube.com/watch?v=hf1h9Ts5fh0**

Carolyn Rose:

Youtube.com/watch?v=xoy3vNUjLOU&t=3s

Loneliness is non-existent in the RV world

RVers are a friendly bunch, and you will be welcomed into the tribe whether you're camping in an RV park or with a few RVers out in the boondocks.

So, don't let the fact that you will be traveling solo be a reason not to enjoy the RV lifestyle.

When you realize that loneliness and security are not a problem for solo RVers, what else is there to worry about?

I'm convinced that solo RVers are safer traveling and living in their rigs than they would be in conventional homes. And I know they're having more fun. I know I am for sure.

Bottom line—what I wish I had known 7 years ago: When I first started RVing, seven years ago, all I saw were couples traveling around in their RVs. I thought I didn't fit in. I didn't even have a dog. I soon found out that whether you're solo or traveling with someone, it doesn't matter. Sitting around the campfire everyone wants to talk to you—maybe even more so than they want to talk to couples. Solo RVing seems to be a plus instead of a minus.

I wish I had known all of this when I started. I wouldn't have wasted so much time feeling out of place in campgrounds.

Chapter 8

10 Wonderful Gadgets I Didn't Know About

"Live life with no excuses, travel with no regret."

~ Oscar Wilde

About the only thing that limits what you can add to your RV is your budget.

I've made modifications and added several things to my motorhome in the seven years I've been on the road. Some of them have been expensive and some have been dirt cheap. Here are some things you might want to put on your Christmas or birthday wish list.

I haven't shown pictures of all of these items, but I have provided links so you can click and see pictures and more information about the items on Amazon.

Here is my list of what I would call my ten favorite gadgets or modifications:

1. **Tire pressure monitor:**
   https://www.amazon.com/dp/B00EHHV2OU TST 507rv Tire Monitor System $310 for a six-sensor system.

   There are several brands of tire pressure monitoring systems on the market and I haven't heard anything bad about any of them. The one referenced here from Truck System Technologies is the only one I've had experience with. I love it. Having a digital readout on the dash showing the air pressure and temperature of all six tires on my motorhome, plus the tires on my dolly and back tires on my car when I'm towing it, is worth its weight in gold to me.

   At a price of a little over $300, it's expensive, but I can easily justify the expense by using my tires for at least one year longer than I would without the system. In other words, using that kind of accounting, I can consider the system to be free.

2. **EternaBond RSW-4-50** roof sealant tape: Use it to cover seams on your roof and it will never leak again. A 50ft

roll of 4-inch wide tape is $52 on Amazon. Here is the link: **https://www.amazon.com/dp/B002RSIK4G**

Flex Seal has come out with their brand of tape called Flex Tape to prevent leaks. I used some yesterday and it was easy to work with. At this time, I don't have a preferred brand.

3. **Screen door cross bar:** I don't know why all RVs don't come with this as a standard feature. It makes getting in and out a lot easier and it makes the screen door sturdier. It's $18 on Amazon. Here is the link: **https://www.amazon.com/dp/B0012GTVVA**

4. **Handheld moisture meter:** I use this digital moisture tester to know if and when I have leaks. You can quickly find out if you have a leak by checking the moisture in the walls. By all means use one of these when you're checking out an RV to buy. It's $29 on Amazon and here is the link: **https://www.amazon.com/dp/B00275F5O2**

5. **Hardwood floors:** I recently did a major upgrade on my motorhome. The effort was minimal, but the results were major. I ripped out all of the old carpet and replaced it with hardwood flooring. I went with the Rustic Hickory vinyl flooring. To me, hardwood floors look so much cleaner. And they are cleaner. The carpet was never completely clean.

The cost was $300 labor and about $350 for materials. I put the new flooring everywhere—in the bedroom, bathroom, and all over. I used the top-of-the-line vinyl flooring. I could have saved about $100 by using a lower grade of flooring. I'm happy with the results. That's what matters.

6. **Sewer hose:** You might think it would be hard to get excited about a sewer hose, but take a look at this one and you might get excited too. I leave it connected to my motorhome and I just open the door, grab the end of the hose and stick it in the dump fitting and use the handle to open the valve. (Of course, I have to open the valve back at the tank too.) It's the Lippert 359724 Waste Master 20-foot Extension RV Sewer Hose Management System for $124. Here's the link to it on Amazon:
   https://www.amazon.com/dp/B010X65OHE
7. **Oxygenics shower head and hose:** This shower head uses very little water and it feels like you're getting a high-pressure stream of water. It's great for rinsing your hair. It has a lifetime warranty. It's $33 and here's a link to it on Amazon:
   https://www.amazon.com/dp/B00F5MUB66
8. **RV surge protector:** I have the Progressive Industries EMS-PT50X Portable RV Surge Protector 50-amp

model. This model sells for $353 and is available from Amazon at this link:
https://www.amazon.com/dp/B01N9MOY7B

Of course, the 30-amp models are a little less. There are different brands and different models ranging from about $150 to $450. Are these devices worth this much? It's like asking if having collision insurance is worth it. Having low voltage, high voltage or voltage spikes can destroy electronic equipment and air conditioners. If you can afford one, I think they are well worth the money. The models that you wire in permanently are a little less expensive than the portable models.

9. **External holding tank monitoring system:** The SEE LEVEL 709P31003 Tank Monitoring System is a little expensive at $251, and maybe it's not necessary, but if you need something else to put on your wish list, this is a great thing to have.

   Everyone knows that the sensors installed inside the holding tanks on RVs are almost useless and they always give false readings because the sensors are always getting gunked up. This device has sensors that stick to the outside of the tanks, so they can't get contaminated. You get an accurate, digital reading of all three tanks on a monitor panel installed inside your RV. I love mine. Here is a link to it on Amazon:
   https://www.amazon.com/dp/B01N6B5ORH

10. **Kit to use an external propane tank:** This kit allows you to connect an external propane tank to your RV. Instead of having to drive the RV to get your propane tank refilled, you can use an external tank. These kits run between $35 and $85. The kits are easy to install. I have one and love it. Here's a link to one model on Amazon. I think this is the one I have:
    https://www.amazon.com/dp/B0014JG7RQ

11. **This is a bonus item. A battery charge monitoring system:** It constantly monitors the charge going into my batteries and the amount of discharge. It does the calculation and displays how much charge I have left in my batteries. It's very useful when I'm boondocking.

    One of the things I like best about the device is that when I'm boondocking and I want to run my generator to charge my battery bank, without this device I never know when the batteries are fully charged.

    You can't just measure the battery voltage and tell. You can if you wait a few hours until the surface charge dissipates. An easy way to picture this is to think about a mug of beer. You have to wait until the foam head has dissipated before you can know how much beer is really in the mug.

    The one I use is the **Victron BMV-702 Battery Monitor**. You can get it at Amazon at the link below for $179.

The model BMV-700 is a little less expensive at $148. The only difference is that it doesn't have the battery temperature sensor.

https://www.amazon.com/dp/B00MJ85E2U

As you can see, some of these items are for your safety, some are for preventing damage to your RV and equipment, some items are for peace of mind, and some are for enjoyment or convivence (shower head and sewer hose).

I like them all but then I'm a gadget freak. Well, I don't know if I'm a freak, but being an engineer, I do like gadgets.

Bottom line—what I wish I had known 7 years ago: If I had known about all of these gadgets seven years ago, I would have started accumulating them sooner. Your RV may already have some of these items and if it doesn't, your budget may not allow you to purchase all of them at once but look at the list and, as your budget allows, start accumulating the ones you think would be the most beneficial to you.

Chapter 9

Myths, Misconceptions, and Downright Lies

"Reality called, so I hung up."

~ Anonymous

There are a lot of myths, misconceptions and downright lies floating around about living full time in an RV.

There are some things you need to be concerned about when you're living full-time in a RV (or when you're considering it), but make sure you're concerned about real problems and not untrue ones.

There is a lot of information glorifying the RVing lifestyle and making it sound like it's all sunsets, campfires, and margaritas.

There is also information out there that make it sound like living the full-time RVing lifestyle is a horrible mistake and something you will regret if you try it.

In the rest of this chapter I want to debunk what I consider to be the seven most prominent untrue myths about the RV lifestyle.

#1. RVs are expensive and a financial disaster. You'll lose your shirt if you buy an RV because they depreciate like mad. This could happen if you buy a new RV and then sell it in a year or two. New RVs depreciate like mad. You should never buy a new RV as your first RV.

When you visit an RV dealership, it's easy to fall in love with one of those new, shiny RVs. On top of that, with payments stretched out over 20 years, new RVs can seem downright affordable.

The problem is that almost all RVers decide they want a different RV after a year or two on the road. I have friends who have had four different types of RVs in the three years they've been on the road. They didn't lose their shirt because they bought each of their RVs at an attractive price. They made a profit on each of the three RVs they have sold.

When you first start living the RV life you don't know much about RVs, so how could you pick the right one for you?

The second problem is that even if you do a lot of research and become somewhat of an expert on RVs, you will probably still buy the wrong RV because how you want to live will most likely change.

So yes, buying an RV can be expensive and it can be a financial disaster. That is IF you buy a new RV and then want to sell it in a year of two.

The truth is that if you buy a used (even a very used) RV, do your research and find an RV that's priced below its market value, and you do a good job of negotiating (how to do all of this was explained in Chapter 3), you can buy an RV, keep it a year of two and possibly sell it and make a profit. I know plenty of people who have done this.

Whether buying an RV is expensive and a financial disaster or not depends on how you go about it. For some people that has proven to be the case. Don't let it happen to you.

#2. Full-time RVing is for retired or rich people only. Not true. A recent industry report said that 40% of the RVs sold last year were sold to young, non-retired people.

A few years ago, it was true that RVers were mostly retired people and a few trust-fund kids, but not anymore. There are a lot of young people and people who are not necessarily young, but not retired, and not rich, who are living full-time in their RVs.

There are two main reasons why this is happening.

#1. There is a staggering amount of information on the internet (in the form of blogs and YouTube videos) and a lot of books available that tell people about the lifestyle. Other RVers explain how they're doing it, how they're making money (and yes, in many cases, making the lifestyle sound more fun and glamorous than it really is). Just a few years ago, this information was not available. If you didn't know someone personally who was living full time in an RV, information about the lifestyle and how to go about it was hard to come by. That's no longer the case.

#2. The second reason young and non-retired people are hitting the road in RVs is that they can live inexpensively on the road, and it's easy to make more money than it's costing them to live the RVing lifestyle. The internet has now made it possible to make a good living while not having what is considered a real job. Chapter 15 shows you how RVers are making money while enjoying life in their RVs.

Not only can you make money doing work on your computer, but you can use your computer to find what is called "workamping" jobs where you do physical labor (campground hosts, picking fruit and vegetables, working in shops, being a waiter or waitress) and the list of optional ways to make money goes on and on.

You can also sell things on eBay, Amazon, Etsy, etc. I guess that would be a combination of physical work and computer work.

Thinking that you can't afford to live full time in an RV is no longer a reason not to do it. You can likely live in an RV and put more money into savings than you did when you were working your full-time nine to five job (I know I do). You probably won't make as much as you're making now, but your living expenses can be reduced considerably by taking advantage of boondocking and other free camping options.

#3. Extremely low gas mileage makes RV travel almost prohibitive. It's true that RVs don't get great gas mileage. I get about eight mpg in my 34-foot, Class A motorhome when I'm towing my car. Smaller RVs get a lot better gas mileage, but let's use my beast of a gas-hog as a worst-case example.

I've seen gas priced below $2.00 a gallon in several places lately. At eight mpg and gas priced at $2.00 a gallon, that's 25 cents a mile or $25 to drive 100 miles.

If you travel all the time, want to take a trip to Alaska or want to visit every national park in one year, you could rack up some miles, but most RVers don't do that. Some travel a lot the first year, but then they realize that RVing is more enjoyable if they slow down.

I like to stay in one place for at least a month. If I stay in one place for a month and then drive 200 miles to the next place, that would mean that I would be spending $50 a month on gas. Even if I only stayed in one place for one week and then drove 200 miles to my next location, I would be driving 800 miles a month and spending $200 a month on gas. You may be spending more than $200 a month on gas now.

The truth is that what you'll spend on gas as a full-time RVer is almost a non-issue. To make things even better, you can cut your gas expenses down to zero for a month or two anytime you want to by just not driving. You don't have to always be driving. When you find a place you like, you can stay and enjoy the area. That's what I do. Also, your next location is probably not going to be 200 miles away.

#4. Live the RVing lifestyle and your problems will go away. A lot of RVing videos, blogs, and books make living the RV lifestyle sound like it would make all your problems go away. Not so. It could even add to your problems. RVing won't change who you are.

For example, if you and your spouse don't get along, you will probably not get along as well as you do now if you start living in an RV. If you're having financial problems, you will continue to have financial problems unless you change the way you spend money.

When you start living the RV lifestyle is a great time to get rid of a lot of baggage (both literally and figuratively). It's a good time to make changes to your life, but don't expect the changes to happen automatically.

If you want things in your life to change, you must make the effort to change them. The RV won't make the changes for you.

#5. RVs are way too small for full-time living. When people start thinking about downsizing from a house to an RV, they usually think they need a big RV.

The truth is that most people who have been RVing for very long realize that their RV is way too big (me included). When buying their second RV, almost everyone I know has gone to a smaller RV.

For example, after five years on the road living in a17-foot Casita camper, Becky Schade, (author of the RV blog, https://interstellarorchard.com) sold her "big" 17-foot camper and bought a 13-foot teardrop type camper. The smaller camper allows her to get to more remote boondocking places.

Of all the things you need to consider and be concerned with, your RV being too small to live in comfortably, will not be one of them, at least not after you have lived in your RV for a while.

You probably don't believe me now, but take my word for it and move on to worrying about something else.

#6. Trying to RV with kids is a nightmare. A lot of RVing families disagree with this statement. They love the amount of time they get to spend with their kids and getting to watch them grow up. They wouldn't want to live any other way.

You can RV if you have kids—here's how

Kids adjust well to life on the road. They experience so much more of life and of the real world than they ever would in a classroom or living in a typical neighborhood. With home-schooling and the internet, traveling with kids (of any age) is a very viable option.

Here are some videos that will let you see for yourself what RVing with kids is like.

- **Youtube.com/watch?v=z4QSp28ymvQ** – Nate, Marissa, and their young daughter enjoying the RVing lifestyle.
- **Youtube.com/watch?v=BsEs-CLBbaU&t-98s** – Marc and Tricia travel with their kids and have posted several fun, interesting, and informative RVing videos.

- **Youtube.com/watch?v=c2xkfkhfcEg** – Nate and Christian Axness are a young couple who travel with their two kids. I think you will find their videos interesting. Here's another one of their videos: **Youtube.com/watch?v=xKLparutJhk&t=149s**

- On December 4th, 2016, Brittany and Eric brought Caspian (or baby nomad as they sometimes call him) home from the hospital and moved him into their Class A motorhome when he was one day old. If you want to know more about how this is working out, you can follow them on their blog at **RVwanderlust.com/one-year-old-rv**

Things to consider when RVing with kids

It's important that each child has his own space. In addition to having his own bed, it's important for each child to have a special place to store personal stuff. Personal space is important. It doesn't have to be big, but it does need to be entirely the child's place.

If you're traveling with teenagers, it may be a little more difficult to make them happy about leaving their friends back home. It can be helpful to involve the older kids in making the plans for where to go next. Maybe even have them go online and make reservations and map out routes and decide where to stop along the way.

Another thing that older kids enjoy from time to time is to have one or two of their friends come along for a week or so. If there's not enough room in the RV, pitch a tent next to it.

With the internet, Skype, Facebook, email, etc., kids can stay in touch with their friends and they'll have so many interesting adventures to share with them. Some kids even start their own blog so their friends can keep up with them.

YouTube has lots of videos that have been posted by RVers who are living the RV lifestyle with their kids. Watch some of them and see how they do it.

Here are some more videos showing people RVing with kids. I recommend that you watch these videos if you are thinking about RVing with kids.

- **Youtube.com/watch?v=nq5s15uuG34**
- **Youtube.com/watch?v=xjixHDkYwPw**

Search YouTube for "RVing with kids" (or some similar phrase) and you will find a ton of videos about RVing with kids of all ages—from toddlers to teenagers.

Below are two of my favorite short videos where young couples explain how they RV with their young child and why they wouldn't want to live or raise a child in a conventional house and be working a nine-to-five job.

- Vimeo.com/71385845 — In this seven-minute video you will see why this couple chose to sell their house and most of their stuff so they could travel and raise their kid while living a non-traditional lifestyle.
- https://www.youtube.com/watch?v=qP1bXCifg_8&t=2s — Nathan and Marissa, have been on the road three more years since this four-minute video was posted. They have gone from the large Class A RV shown in this video to a much smaller Airstream camper. And by the way, the 18-month-old little girl (who is now four) in this video is going to have a brother or sister in a few months. If you want to know even more about their lifestyle, check out their other videos on YouTube. Their YouTube channel is called, *Less Junk—More Journey.*

What if you have more than one kid?

Here is a link to Michael and Laine's YouTube video explaining how they live full time in their RV with four kids.

- **https://www.youtube.com/watch?v=innUlndRr54**

Below is a link to a YouTube video showing how Mike and Megan live full-time in their RV with nine kids.

- **https://www.youtube.com/watch?v=GYwO4UX6tc0**

One thing is for sure, kids who grow up living in an RV get exposed to a whole different world. They also learn to be outgoing (since they are meeting new people all the time), and since they are being home-schooled, they are not exposed to drugs like they are in public schools—that's just my observations and two cents' worth.

#7. RV repair costs will eat you alive. RV repair costs can get expensive if you have all your repair work done at an RV repair shop. Check out Chapter 12 and you will see how RVers save a lot of money on their RV repairs. Take a close look at this chapter before you decide that RV repair costs will eat you alive.

#8. People who live in RVs are broke and can't afford a house. This is a bonus myth that I wanted to explain. RVers no longer worry about keeping up with the Joneses. It doesn't matter whether you have a $3,000 RV or a $300,000 RV. Surprisingly, some people who live and travel in a $3,000 RV could easily afford a $300,000 RV.

There are a few RVers who live in an RV because they can't afford a house, but most RVers live in an RV by choice and not by necessity. You won't find riff-raff in RV parks or in boondocking areas.

Just because many RVers spend a lot of time camping in boondocking areas (national parks, on government owned BLM land, and in other free camping areas), it's not because they can't afford to pay and camp in an RV park. It's just that they are being frugal. And besides, I've experienced some of the most fun and enjoyable camping when boondocking.

Bottom line—what I wish I had known 7 years ago: I wish I had realized that a lot of the things you hear from non-RVers are not true. Take comments about RVing from people who have never been there and done that with a grain of salt.

I'm sure most of them don't mean to be saying things that are myths, misconceptions, or downright lies. They're just repeating what they have been told by other uninformed non-RVers.

Chapter 10

Controlling Expenses

"It's tough to make predictions, especially about the future."

~ Yogi Berra

After I made the decision that I was going to hit the road and live full time in an RV one way or another, I started getting serious about working out a budget.

I was looking at my estimated expenses and income, and I was allowing for emergencies and unforeseen things to happen. I had an emergency fund, but I wondered what would happen if I had two emergencies back to back.

Being an engineer, I like to look at things in a logical way. I know that just because some random, unexpected event happens it doesn't make it any less likely to happen again.

I had an otherwise intelligent friend tell me after he had experienced a once in a 100-year flood, "At least I don't have to worry about that happening again for another 100 years." That's not how it works with random events.

I've heard people in a casino say that they are due to roll a seven because they have rolled the dice 10 times since they last rolled a seven. Again, it doesn't work that way.

What has happened prior to a random event doesn't have anything to do with the next event.

I knew my emergency fund could cover a blown engine, but what if I had my transmission go out the next week? Just because you have had one bad (and expensive) random event happen to you, it doesn't lower your chances of another one happening.

If it did, insurance companies would lower your insurance rates after you have an auto accident because they would reason that you would not likely have another accident anytime soon. It doesn't work that way.

I think you are beginning to see the folly of this way of thinking.

By the way, my uncle and aunt had a 100-year flood damage their house three years in a row. Go figure.

The reason I'm going over this is because, in order to reduce stress, you must plan for emergencies, and you have to realize that emergencies are random events that can happen at any time.

You need an emergency fund, but you also need a backup plan in case you use up all or most of your emergency fund. You would like to have an option other than dipping into your savings or investments.

I worried about this scenario a lot. I wish I had known how other RVers deal with this situation. I found out that the simple solution is that RVers can greatly reduce their living expenses at the drop of a hat.

They can boondock and cut their camping fees to zero for a while, and they can stop traveling and not go anywhere so their gas expense will be zero. When they're boondocking, they can go hiking and do other fun and interesting things and not spend any money on entertainment.

You can't do any of these things when you live in a typical stick-and-brick house or apartment. You can't stop paying rent or stop paying your mortgage, and you can't stop driving to work.

Another option is that you can also pick up another income-producing gig. You may only be getting minimum wage at the new gig, but you can do it for a month or so, and it could be interesting and enjoyable.

With one or two months of greatly reduced expenses and some extra cash coming in, you can replenish an emergency fund in short order.

You probably will never need to take actions this drastic, but just knowing that you can do these things any time you need to can take a lot of stress off you.

Bottom line—what I wish I had known 7 years ago: I wish I had known how easy it would be to drastically cut my living expenses and how easy it would be to immediately start bringing in extra income if I ever needed it. I probably wouldn't necessarily want to do either of these things long-term, but for a month or two, I could take these steps and enjoy the adventure. I wish I had known about these options seven years ago.

Chapter 11

Getting Rid of Stuff

"A house is just a place to keep your stuff while you go out and get more stuff."

~ George Carlin

Stuff is the killer of joy. Most people agree with this statement until it's time for them to get rid of their stuff.

I dreaded having to tackle this problem until I finally had to face the facts and start getting rid of my stuff. After I made up my mind to do it, I realized that it was so much easier than I had imagined.

I wish I had known how easy it would be to get rid of stuff. At least, it was easy to do after I made the decision to actually do it.

When you're getting ready to hit the road and live in an RV, there is one problem everyone faces—what to do with all the somewhat valuable junk they have accumulated.

Now is the perfect time to get rid of a lot of clutter in your home and your life. Before you start living the RVing life, get rid of a lot of baggage (both literally and figuratively).

I hear people say things all the time such as, "I could never live in an RV. I have too much stuff."

They say it with the same conviction they would say one leg was longer than the other one. They act like they were born with all the stuff and there is nothing they can do about the situation.

When you get rid of all the useless junk (I mean valuable stuff) you have accumulated, you open up so many options for how you want to live your life. If you're tied down by stuff, your options are limited.

Get rid of your junk and then you're free to hit the road and live in an RV.

If you need even more help, I wrote a book called *Tidying Up.* In addition to showing you how to tidy up once and for all and never have to do it again, the book also shows you how to decide what to get rid of.

The full title of the book is *Tidying Up: The Magic and Secrets of Decluttering Your Home and Your Life*

Since you're trying to get rid of stuff, you don't need another book around the house. As it says in the book, buy mostly eBooks from now on and there is an eBook version of this book available. The eBook version is available from Amazon for $3.99 at the link below:

Amazon.com/dp/B01J6EVSR4

Read and follow the rest of this chapter and you probably won't need to buy the book, but if you need extra help, the book can be your plan "B".

How to get rid of your stuff

Consider the following story to help you understand the concept.

A friend of mine told me that when she decided to live full time in an RV, she wasn't ready to get rid of all her stuff, so she stored everything that wouldn't fit in her RV in a barn on her parents' farm.

About a year later, the barn caught fire, and everything was destroyed. She said she should have been devastated, but she found herself feeling happy and didn't know why.

Then she realized the reason she was happy was that all her stuff was gone, and she didn't have to feel guilty for getting rid of any of it. (The things she really wanted she had taken with her.)

It wasn't that she wanted any of the stuff. She just didn't want to get rid of it at the time. I think that describes a lot of us.

If you say, "I choose to have all of this stuff," then you own the situation or problem. It's easier to deal with the situation when you look at it that way.

Here are the steps to getting rid of your stuff

Your stuff can all be classified into one of four categories, A, B, C, and D.

Category A: Things you are going to use and take with you. (If you're like most RVers, later you'll end up getting rid of a lot of the stuff you thought you had to have.)

Category B: These are the things you can sell—your dining room table and chairs, the sofa you bought two years ago, your riding lawnmower. You can sell almost everything, and it doesn't take long to do it. Selling all this stuff is a good way to bring in some extra cash.

Craigslist is a great way to sell larger items. If you price the items right and include pictures, they will usually sell within a week. If an item doesn't sell within a week, lower the price by at least a third and list it again.

Be sure to list a phone number where you can be reached most of the time. When someone is ready to buy something, if they can't get you on the phone, they will call another person selling essentially the same type of item you're offering.

I have sold a lot of items using Craigslist. The system works great. You get a fair price, and you get it sold quickly.

For smaller items that you can ship, you can use eBay. For both Craigslist and eBay, be sure to show several good quality pictures. Pictures help items sell quickly. With eBay, you can set a reserve price or you can auction it off and take what you get. After all, usually, whatever it sells for is what it's worth, and that's what you wanted to do in the first place—sell the item for whatever it's worth.

Category C: These are the things that you put in a garage sale on a Saturday and then take what doesn't sell to Goodwill. This way, at the end of the day, everything in this category is gone.

Category D: This category is for sentimental things. A few of these things you may want to put in storage but very few. Pictures and photo albums can all be scanned and put on a thumb drive. If you don't know how to do this, there are businesses that offer this service at a reasonable price.

Most people think things on this list are the hardest to get rid of, but, in fact, these items can be the easiest to get rid of if you follow the procedure described below.

First, decide who you want to have each of these things when you're dead and gone. (I know you consider that to be a long way off but think about it this way anyway.) Then give the items to them now. If they won't take the things now, you know what will happen to them as soon as you're gone. They'll give them to Goodwill, sell them in a garage sale or throw them away. If you have a few items that you want your grandchildren to have when they're grown, you can put these items in storage if you can't convince their parents to keep the items for them.

I know that it's hard to accept the fact that a lot of things you cherish will not even be considered worth keeping by other people when you're gone. That's just a fact. Don't blame your kids or your relatives. It's not their responsibility or duty to like or value the same things you like.

A lot of the things you will be giving people will be things they will love and really enjoy having. By giving them the items now, you'll get to see them enjoy the things and you'll know the items went to the people you wanted to have them.

Don't just put things in storage—at least not more than what will fit in the smallest storage unit they make.

If you do put things in a storage unit, consider getting rid of even those things a year from now. Some people have found it easier to get rid of sentimental things in a two-step process like this, but don't let it drag out for years and still have your belongings in storage.

In other words, put the things you think you just can't part with in storage for one year. At the end of a year, decide if you want to continue your adventuresome lifestyle. If so, give everything that's in storage that you're not going to use to your relatives. If they don't want it, sell it. If it doesn't sell, give it to Goodwill or throw it away.

It will feel like a tremendous burden is lifted from your shoulders when you have gotten rid of all the stuff you don't need.

There is some wiggle room

Now that I've convinced you to get rid of most of your stuff and shown you how to do it, let me back up and tell you that you do have a little bit of wiggle room.

Many RVers get a small storage unit, and they keep a few things that they're not ready to get rid of yet.

I know one couple who took a picture of their empty storage unit and then threw a party and invited their friends to help them celebrate the big occasion. It was a fun time.

Plan your party now to celebrate your freedom from STUFF!

You have all this stuff because you choose to have it. Therefore, you can choose to get rid of it. You may not believe it now, but it's such a big relief when you get rid of all the stuff you've been hanging on to for years.

One final point: Don't go through your stuff and decide what to throw away. Go through it and decide what to keep. That's important. The best way to decide what to keep is to ask yourself, *Does this bring me joy?* If you're truthful with yourself, you'll decide that most items don't really bring you any joy, so don't keep them. It's that simple.

Bottom line—what I wish I had known 7 years ago: I fretted a lot about getting rid of most of my stuff. What I wish I had known was how easy it would be to get rid of most of my accumulated junk once I decided on a plan (which is what I've outlined in this chapter). Following these steps made the whole process easy. If I had realized this earlier, I could have saved myself a lot of worry and frustration.

Chapter 12

Repairs and Preventative Maintenance

"It is better to have loafed and lost than to never have loafed at all."

~ James Thurber

RV maintenance can get expensive. At $150 or more an hour, which most RV repair shops charge, it doesn't take long to run up a large repair bill even for a minor repair problem.

I paid $459 one time to have a radiator hose clamp replaced. Ouch. When I first started RVing, I had all my repair work done at an RV repair shop.

I was always afraid that if I tried to do the work myself and got something taken apart, I might not get it fixed or put back together, and then what would I do? I would be up the proverbial creek without the proper population. (That's not the words normally used to describe that situation.)

Two ways I now save money on RV repairs

#1. Mobile RV repair techs. Mobile RV techs are not cheap. They charge $75 to $95 an hour, but that's a lot better than the $150 an hour RV repair shops charge.

In addition to the lower rate, another thing I like about mobile RV repair technicians is that I can watch what they're doing. This way I can learn and maybe the next time I can fix the problem myself.

When you take your RV to an RV repair shop, you don't get to go back in the shop and watch the mechanic.

#2. Watching YouTube videos. Most of the time when I have an RV repair problem, the first thing I do now is look at some YouTube videos describing how to fix the problem. I like to watch two or three different videos posted by different people. You can go to YouTube and search for the keywords describing your problem and usually find several videos with information about how to solve your problem.

One series of videos that I find particularly helpful can be found at:

Youtube.com/user/RVgeeks

You can go to this link and then search for the keywords that describe your problem and they usually have a video showing you how to fix your problem. They have been full-time RVers for 15 years and have produced hundreds of YouTube videos.

You can also find great RV repair articles on their website at

www.TheRVgeeks.com

You've probably read the book by Richard Carlson, *Don't Sweat the Small Stuff—and It's All Small Stuff.* The book was written more than 20 years ago, but the information and advice in the book still applies to situations today.

When it comes to RV repair jobs, it's true that most things that need to be fixed are small things. You probably won't have any trouble with your engine, transmission or drivetrain in general.

You will have problems with things such as the spring in the door latch, a roof leak, windshield wiper blades, a broken string in a window blind, a leak under the kitchen sink or the water pump stops working (the coach water pump, not the engine water pump). I know because these are all things I've had to fix or replace recently.

I'm glad I didn't have to pay an RV repair shop $150 an hour to fix these problems. None of these problems would have left me stranded beside the road, and none of them required immediate attention.

Sometimes the fact that a minor problem doesn't have to be fixed immediately can mean that it gets put off forever and ever. Ask me how I know this.

Bottom line—what I wish I had known 7 years ago: I wish I had known about mobile RV repair services and I also wish I had known that there were YouTube videos that show how to do most types of RV repairs. Of course, there were not as many YouTube videos available seven years ago as there are now, but I'm sure there were some. If I had known about these two simple things, I would have saved a lot of money over the years.

Chapter 13

Mail, Healthcare, and Misc. Information

"Fear is only temporary. Regrets last forever."

~ Anonymous

You have probably been giving a lot of thought and time to some of the things that are considered to be the bigger problems and tasks required to hit the road and live full time in an RV—things like finding and buying the right RV, selling your house, getting rid of most of your stuff, etc.

Of course, these big things are important, but there are some little things that are important too. Here are some tasks that don't take much time, but they are easy to put off. And sometimes you can completely forget to take care of them.

Don't fall into the trap of putting these things off. Make a list and start knocking them out.

Most of the information in the rest of this chapter is things I have written about in the articles on my website (**www.LifeRV.com**) and in some of my previous RV books. I'm repeating the information here because these things are important, and I want to make sure you consider them before you hit the road.

Six little things to take care of before you hit the road

- In which state is your domicile? In other words, where do you legally live?
- How to get your mail
- How to get healthcare
- How to stay connected to the internet
- How to handle your banking
- What about pets? (Of course, this only applies if you have a pet or are thinking about getting a pet.)

The good news is that there are simple solutions to each of the things I've listed. In the rest of this chapter, I will show you how other RVers have handled each of these problems.

In which state is your domicile (where do you legally live)?

This is the first thing you need to take care of. You can't decide how to get your mail, how to get healthcare, and a lot of other things until you decide where you legally and officially live (even though you may not physically be there very often).

Since you'll probably be rambling all over the US (or at least in several different states), where do you legally live? You can't just say, "Everywhere," even though that might be the correct answer.

You have to declare a state and say it is your domicile, and you have to have a physical address in that state.

Before you can get your driver's license and register your car and motorhome, etc., you have to select a state to call home.

Since it's possible to select any state, most people choose either Texas, Florida or South Dakota because there is no state income tax in these states (along with several other reasons).

There are other states with no income tax, but, for several reasons, Texas and Florida are the two states most RVers choose.

South Dakota used to be a popular state, but they have changed some laws, and it's no longer a good choice in my opinion, particularly if you're not on Medicare.

After you select your domicile state, you will have to do things just as you would if you physically moved there—get a local address, get your driver's license issued in that state, register your vehicles, change your address with all of your credit cards, banks, etc. It's not hard, just a lot of little things to do.

Here is a link to a 43-minute YouTube video by Bob Wells:

Youtube.com/watch?v=jntFI_5FiA8&t=13s
CheapRVLiving.com.

He gives a detailed explanation of your domicile state options and he goes over several things you will want to consider before you select your domicile state. It's a long video and maybe you don't want to know that much about the topic right now, but, at some point, before you make your decision, I would recommend that you watch it.

By the way, the choice Bob made for where to call home works for him (and he explains why), but for most people, I would recommend FL or TX instead of the choice he made.

Keep in mind that, out of the three main full-time residency states (Florida, Texas, and South Dakota) only Florida has Obamacare plans that provide nationwide coverage (Florida Blue). This may change later in 2019.

One other point to keep in mind is that if you presently live in an aggressive tax state (such as NY, CA, IL, etc.) and if there is a lot of tax involved, these states may come after you and try to claim that you are still a resident of their state and therefore owe them tax revenue. In some cases, they have been successful at this.

It comes down to which state you plan to eventually live in. It might be hard to convince tax authorities that you plan to live permanently in South Dakota when you have only been there once in five years.

After considering all of these options, I would suggest that you seriously consider Florida as your domicile state, but it's not the best option for everyone. Consider everything that's been presented here, do your research to see how the rules have changed, and then make your decision.

One other option (and the one a lot of people choose) is to do nothing and keep your domicile state the same as it is now. In other words, use a friend or relative's address or set up a UPS box as your official address.

That's what I did. I left my domicile state as NC. My brother picks up my mail for me about once a month and lets me know if there is anything important (like a summons for jury duty, etc.).

If you plan on going back to your present home state often, this might be the best choice. After all, you can see your same doctors, dentist, auto mechanic, and old friends, etc. on your return visits.

By the way, the State of NC would not let me use my UPS box as the address on my driver's license. Their computer kicked it out, so I had to use my brother's address. No big problem. Just one more hoop to have to jump through.

I still have to pay NC state income tax. I might decide to change to Florida one of these days, but for the last seven years, I have continued to officially live in NC.

One of the reasons I have been thinking about establishing my official domicile state as Florida is that, in addition to not having to pay any state income tax, Florida residents can stay in Florida state parks for half price, which is about $9 a night and that includes water and electricity.

Another reason I haven't changed yet is that it's expensive the first year to transfer vehicle registrations (motorhome and car) to Florida. After the first year, it's relatively inexpensive.

How do you get your mail?

After you select a state to call home, you will need an address in that state, so you need to establish an address with a friend or a mail forwarding service.

If you have a friend or relative in the state you select, you might want to consider using them and their address to save a little money.

Here are some links to recommended mail forwarding services in each of the three common states people choose as their domicile. Contact them and they can give you many more details.

Florida:

SbiMailService.com

Escapees.com

MyRvMail.com

AmHomeBase.com

Texas:

Escapees.com

South Dakota:

Americas-Mailbox.com

These mail forwarding services charge a small monthly fee (about $15 to $25 a month) depending on the services you want them to perform. For example, they will forward all of your mail when you request it (weekly, monthly, etc.). You will have to give them an address each time you want your mail forwarded.

They also offer a service to scan the outside of your mail and email the scans to you and then you can tell them which pieces to forward and which ones to trash.

For an extra fee, they will even open your mail and scan the contents and email that to you.

I would suggest you take steps to eliminate as much of your snail mail as possible. It just makes life easier. One easy way to eliminate a lot of unwanted mail is not to file a forwarding address with your current post office. That will eliminate a lot of junk mail. Give your new address only to the people and businesses you want to have it.

Now that you've decided on your domicile state, the next step is to take the necessary steps to actually get an address set up in that state. You have to do this before you can start getting healthcare set up.

When you have an address, you can start getting your vehicle registration and insurance changed over and, of course, start jumping through the hoops to get health insurance, which I will describe next—but you have to select a domicile state and have an address before you can do any of this.

Of course, be sure to change your address with the IRS, your banks, your eBay, and Amazon account, and anywhere else that's important.

How will you get healthcare?

How you're going to get healthcare and health insurance for you and your family is one of the most important things you need to make a decision about and then make it happen before you hit the road.

Health insurance costs and options have changed a lot lately and will probably change more by the time you read this, so rather than me trying to give you the latest information on health insurance, I'm going to give you some general information and also provide you with links showing you where you can get the absolute latest information and learn about the best options for you and your situation.

Getting healthcare when you don't live in one place can be difficult and expensive.

The major problem is finding a healthcare plan that doesn't restrict you to doctors in your network.

If you are old enough to be on Medicare, it's a lot easier because Medicare covers you in all 50 states.

One important point: If you are on Medicare, do NOT change to a Medicare Advantage plan because these have a network of doctors and you will likely be out of the network area a lot of the time. Keep your original Medicare and purchase one of the Medicare Supplement plans. These cover you in all 50 states.

If you're not old enough to be on Medicare, I suggest you hurry up and get old enough and your insurance problems will be a lot easier.

In the meantime, there are other options.

Here are some things to consider before you sign up for a health insurance plan

- Some insurance companies flatly don't insure RVers. Avoid these.
- Some plans require you to live in the state for at least six months out of the year. Avoid these.
- Avoid HMO plans and stick with PPO plans that have a large nationwide network of providers.

One of the best places to get up-to-date information is on Kyle Henderson's website:

RVerInsurance.com

Kyle is a full-time RVer himself. Here is a link that will take you straight to the page on his website that has the latest health insurance information and options.

RVerInsurance.com/health-insurance

In addition to the above information here are three other websites that provide some useful information about healthcare:

- **HealthSherpa.com** — This site allows you to do comparison shopping of exchange policy plans.
- **24-7healthInsurance.com** — Coleen Elkins is one of the best in the business when it comes to health insurance information for those under 65. Check out her website or call her at 888-337-1705. She is licensed in 11 states including FL, TX, and SD. You should probably set up your domicile state to be one of these states as I've described previously.
- **RVerhiexchange.com**

An option to consider

If you're self-employed, not old enough for Medicare, and are basically in good health, here's an option you should consider. Have a plan with **Healthcare.gov**, which is commonly called the Marketplace.

I've seen payments from zero (yes, zero) up to $50 a month depending on which state you're in, what subsidy level you qualify for, and other factors. This is doable even on a limited budget.

If you're only working part time and not making much money, your subsidy level for Affordable Care Act insurance is going to get your out-of-pocket payments down to almost nothing—maybe even zero.

There are a lot of differences in the Marketplace offerings of the different states. One important fact to keep in mind is that, of the three states that most full-time RVers select as their domicile state (Texas, South Dakota, and Florida), only Florida (Florida Blue) has Marketplace plans that provide nationwide coverage.

This is important if you have health issues that require you to see your doctor frequently. You wouldn't want to have to drive from California or Georgia to South Dakota every time you needed to see a doctor.

Being able to get nationwide insurance coverage when you're not on Medicare is another reason why I recommend you seriously look at Florida as your domicile state.

For a good summary of health insurance options in 2019 for pre-Medicare RVers, check out the following articles.

Below is a link to an article that Nina Wheeling posted on her blog.

Wheelingit.us/2017/10/31 (Note that this is a dot **us** and NOT a dot **com** address.)

The article was up to date as of Nov. 2017 and does an excellent job of describing and summarizing the current options for RVers who are not yet old enough to be on Medicare. Most of the information is still valid.

Below is an article that Nina posted that was up to date as of Nov. 2018. It covers what has changed since her last post, and there is some good news.

https://wheelingit.us/2018/11/02

Keep in mind that if you missed the signup period, there's a loophole that will allow you to sign up for coverage at any time of the year. The loophole is that when you move to a different state, you can sign up for new coverage. The key is that if you change your domicile state, that's considered moving to a different state.

Having insurance doesn't guarantee that you will get to see a doctor.

Even though you have insurance, getting an appointment to see a doctor in a city where you have never been to a doctor before can sometimes be a problem.

Four techniques RVers use to get to see a doctor when they're on the road

1. Go to an emergency medical clinic.
2. Sign up with **Teladoc.com**. You can place a call and a board-certified doctor will call you back (usually within 10 to 15 minutes). The doctor will discuss your symptoms with you and call in a prescription to a pharmacy near you, or, if necessary, tell you if they think you need to see a specialist.
3. CVS, Walgreens, and some other pharmacies now have a nurse practitioner on staff part of the time. You can walk in; they can examine you and then write a prescription for your minor health problems.
4. Another option is to start calling doctors' offices and see if you can get an appointment to see one in a reasonable time frame. I've used this technique twice in seven years and it has worked out fine. I still go to my doctor back in NC for my annual physicals.

Keep in mind that the health insurance rules and options change from time to time. Some of the things I discussed and linked to in this chapter may have changed by the time you read this, so be sure to do your homework and do a lot of research before you make decisions about which healthcare options are best for you and your situation.

How to connect to the internet

Keep in mind that, even though almost all campgrounds say they have fast, high-speed internet, you may not have a strong signal all over the campground and during peak usage times it can get very slow.

If the internet is really important to you (and it will be if you're using it to make an income), you will probably need another option other than relying on the campground WiFi.

The options I use are hotspot devices. All carriers offer them, and the prices and plans are changing all the time.

Right now, I'm testing three different options. I have a Verizon JetPack, an AT&T Mobley, and a T-Mobile device. I mostly use the AT&T Mobley device because I get unlimited data for $20 a month. Unfortunately, that plan is no longer being offered, but the internet providers continue to introduce new plans all the time. Check to see what plans are available now.

Verizon has the best coverage and T-Mobile has a plan where the data you use watching YouTube, Netflix, and Hulu videos doesn't count against your data usage. In other words, there are advantages and disadvantages to all of your options. On top of that, the carriers are always changing their plans and prices.

When you're ready to hit the road, check out the different carriers and see which one is presently offering the best plan. Also, check their coverage maps to be sure they have good coverage in the areas where you will be traveling the most.

To find out the latest up-to-date RV internet options, I depend on Chris and Cherie. Here is a link to their website:

RVmobileinternet.com/classroom

Here is a link to a YouTube video posted in May of 2018 that summarizes the options they use to connect to the internet.

Youtube.com/watch?v=JcKyAiddQqM&

They provide a lot of free information and they also offer more detailed information if you become a subscriber.

How do you handle banking?

As a full-time RVer, my opinion is that you need accounts with at least two different, unrelated banks. When passwords or debit cards get lost or stolen or when there are problems of any kind with one account, having a second account could save you a lot of grief while you're getting things straightened out.

Also, don't carry all of your credit cards in your wallet. Keep one in your car or RV so if you lose your wallet, you will still have a useable credit card while you're getting your lost one replaced.

Also, when you're looking for a branch bank, if you have two banks you are a lot more likely to find one close to you.

When selecting the two banking institutions, make sure they have branches in the states you plan to travel to the most. I use Wells Fargo and Bank of America, but banks are all rapidly changing the services they offer, so do your homework before selecting your two banks. Online banks are a good option too.

Some features you should look for when selecting banks include the ability to transfer money between accounts online, the ability to make payments online, and the ability to deposit checks by just taking a picture of the check and sending it to them. In other words, you want a bank that is very much into online banking.

You should also keep some cash hidden in your RV. There are lots of places in an RV where you could have a few hundred dollars well hidden.

What about pets and RVs?

In most campgrounds, I would say that about half of the RVs have a dog (or should I say the dog has an RV?). I don't know if any of the dogs actually drive their RV, but most of them seem to be in charge and run the show.

Seriously, pets make great companions when traveling and living the RV lifestyle. They enjoy checking out new places and seeing new things. Even cats that stay inside all of the time seem to enjoy and be intrigued by the new scenery.

Almost all campgrounds allow pets. There are some rules that must be followed, so make sure you and your pet both read the rules. The rules are usually straightforward, common sense rules such as no barking, your dog must be on a leash, clean up after your pet, etc. A few campgrounds don't allow large dogs but most do.

What do you do about healthcare for your pets?

First of all, be sure to keep current copies of all of your pet's vaccinations or you might end up getting duplicate and unnecessary treatments. One solution is to use a national chain of vets such as Banfield Pet Hospital. They have offices all over the country. Go to their website at **Banfield.com** and enter the zip code where you are and you can find their closest office. Many of their offices are located inside PetSmart™ stores. They have a centralized database and your pet's records can be brought up at any of their offices. Wouldn't it be nice if doctors had the same system for us humans?

When traveling with pets, you have to pay a little bit of attention to their special needs—especially when you're away from the RV for a few hours. Make sure it doesn't get too hot or too cold and make sure they have plenty of water.

One last point about traveling with pets

Be sure to keep plenty of your pet's food on hand. You may not be able to find your normal brand everywhere (even if it's a common brand).

Changing your pet's food and then hitting the road in your RV could result in trouble for you and your pet. Don't risk it. Some people order their favorite brand of pet food on Amazon and have it shipped to wherever they are if it's a brand that's not commonly available.

Remember that pets can be expensive

If you already have a dog or a cat, I'm sure you're not going to give it away. But if you don't have a pet and you're trying to live on a low budget, by all means, don't get a pet.

Some RVers tell me that they spend $100 to $200 a month on pet food. Also, vet bills can blow your budget in a heartbeat. A friend just spent $800 on a vet bill, and there was nothing wrong with her dog. It was just for his annual wellness check-up. My brother spent $1,800 on emergency surgery for his little dog because of a blocked bladder.

Having a pet may also interfere with the jobs you can accept. You might not be able to work all day if you have to get back to take your dog out during the day.

Other things you have to deal with when RVing

Voting: You need to get registered to vote. You will vote in the precinct where your legal address is. In some states, you can register to vote when you get your driver's license.

When elections come up, you need to vote in both local and national elections. This will help establish the fact that you are a resident of the state you claim as your domicile. You can vote using an absentee ballot.

Family doctor and dentist: You have to think about whether you want to go back to your present family doctor and dentist for your annual check-ups. That's what I do. A lot of RVers choose to do this. They get to visit with family and friends when they're back in town. Getting back to your former home base at least once a year is something a lot of people look forward to.

You may have been spending most of your time thinking about what kind of RV to buy and how you're going to support yourself when you quit your job, hit the road, and live in an RV, but the little things I've listed above are important, too, and have to be taken care of.

Being away from family and friends is a big deal for some people but take it in stride and realize that you can make it to any of the family reunions or special occasions you want to.

Most major family events are planned way in advance, and you can plan to be there if you really want to. If you're in Arizona and the family reunion or wedding is going to be in Michigan, that could be a problem, but if you plan far enough in advance, you can make it happen.

Don't overlook the option to fly back to family events. Sometimes airfares can be extremely cheap, especially when you purchase them way in advance.

You'll probably want to get back to your former home base from time to time and visit with family and old friends. Plan and make it happen.

Bottom line—what I wish I had known 7 years ago: I wish I had known (or had a list) of all the little things that needed to be taken care of before I hit the road. A lot of these things I took care of after I got on the road, but it would have been easier and better to have taken care of them and made the decisions before I hit the road.

Chapter 14

Other Things You Need to Know

"I need 6 months of vacation, twice a year."

~ Anonymous

In this chapter I'm going to cover a lot of misc. information. I'm sure you will find most of it to be common sense, and think, *Duh, everybody knows that.* Hopefully, you will find one or two gems that you didn't know or hadn't thought of.

Some of these things I knew before I started RVing, so they don't exactly fit in the title of the book about things I wish I had known before I started RVing, but I wanted to include them to give you a more complete understanding of the RVing lifestyle.

If you've read many other RVing books, watched many YouTube videos about living in an RV, or if you're already living in an RV, I'm sure you know most of the following information. My guess is that you will find a few things in this chapter that you didn't know.

Keep in mind that some of these points have been covered in other chapters in this book, but they are worth repeating in a simple, concise statement.

Let's get started.

RVing Words of wisdom in no particular order

- Don't ever leave the black water (sewer) tank valve open. You always want to have water in the black tank.
- You can leave the valve to the gray water tank open since it usually fills up before the black water tank but be sure to close it and let the tank fill at least half full before you drain the black water tank, so you will have gray water available to flush out the hose.
- Always check the air pressure in all of your tires each morning when you're traveling. The first item you should put on your Christmas wish list is a remote tire pressure monitoring system. Having one of these systems will give

you a digital readout on your dashboard of the air pressure of each tire.

- Check your brake lights, turn signals, and fluid levels the day before you are ready to start a trip. The reason for this is that when you're ready to pull out and you check things and find out that a brake light is out, or one turn signal doesn't work, it's tempting to decide that you will head out anyway and fix it when you stop for the night.
- Video the walk-through. Whether you buy your RV from a dealer or an individual, they will do a walk-through and show you how everything works before you leave with your RV. Everything will make sense as they're explaining and demonstrating it, but you won't remember half of it. A day or a week later there will be a lot of things you won't remember how to do. The simple solution is to video the walk-through. I was told to video the walk-through, but I thought I could remember everything. I couldn't, and it caused me a lot of frustration later. Use your cell phone and just do it.
- Take time to smell the roses. Most RVers will tell you that they travelled a lot more their first year on the road than they do now. Even if you want to see every national park, you don't have to see them all immediately. You'll find that the RVing lifestyle is so much more enjoyable

and less stressful if you slow down. Spend some time in places you camp and get to know the area.

- When it's a travel day and I'm just trying to get from point A to point B, I like to spend the night in a Walmart parking lot. It's free, and I don't have to unload the car, disconnect the dolly, and then back into a camping space. I just stop, fix supper, crank up the TV antenna or read, and then the next morning I can pull out and be on my way. I buy a few things from Walmart while I'm there, and I always call the Walmart store before I get there to make sure that it's okay to park there overnight. I also ask where they want me to park. Most Walmart stores allow you to park overnight, but in a few places the city ordinances don't allow it, so be sure to call and ask.
- Have a pre-take-off checklist. It's hard to remember everything. You don't want to be going down the road dragging a sewer hose (I've seen it happen).
- Make sure your RV is level (no more than one bubble off) when you're parked. You can damage (destroy) your refrigerator if it's not level. The ammonia type refrigerators in RVs don't work the same way as the refrigerator in your house that has a compressor.
- Plan to arrive way before dark. Don't push it close. Traffic and other things can make you arrive later than

you planned. By arriving before dark, it's a lot easier to get backed into your space and get set up. Also, I like to look around, and I like to meet my neighbors if they are out and about.

- Don't walk through other people's campsites. It's just not done.
- Don't keep your outside light on all night. It's okay to leave it on when you go out to dinner, so you can see how to find the steps and get back to your RV, but when you get back to your RV, turn the light off. You don't want it shining in the eyes of your neighbors.
- There will be a huge emotional transition. Be prepared for it.
- One of the things I like about the RVing lifestyle is that you meet people who make decisions and make things happen.
- You'll only need one car and you'll stop buying stuff. These two things add up to big savings.
- When you sell your house, you release your emotional ties to the area. This may be good or bad. Think about it.
- When you live in an RV, you have a lot more control over your expenses than you do when living in a traditional stick-and-brick house.

- Why do you want to live the RVing lifestyle? Give this question some serious thought. The answer will help you decide how you go about making the change.
- Moving into an RV won't change who you are or automatically solve all your problems.
- A lot of banks won't finance an RV, so you need to do your homework. It might be easier to get financing before you sell your house. RVs are usually financed for 15 years. Some banks will go up to 20 years on new RVs. Seriously consider buying a used RV for cash as your first RV. Later, when you know more about RVs and what you want, you can consider buying a new RV.
- RV inspections: **PremierRVinspections.com**. This company will almost always find some things wrong and you can use this information to negotiate a lower price. You can usually lower the price by more than what you paid for the inspection, and who knows, the inspector might find something really bad.
- Buy an RV that's way less than you can afford.
- Buy a smaller RV than you think you need or want. Most RVers buy a smaller RV after one or two years on the road. Almost nobody wants a larger RV. There are too many things you can't do if you have a large RV.

- The price of RVs is a lot more negotiable (new or used) than cars. I've seen dealers and individuals drop the asking price of an RV by 30% and in some cases up to 50%.
- You don't need to take as much stuff as you think you need. Most people find out that they don't even need half of the stuff they thought they needed.
- You don't need nearly as many clothes as you think you need. Cut to the bare minimum and you will find that you still don't wear half of what you brought.
- Know the height of your RV (all the way to the top of the air conditioners). Maybe even write it down and post it on your dash until it's etched in your mind. When you see a sign showing the clearance before a tunnel, an overpass or at a gas station is NOT the time to wonder how high your RV is.
- Don't be afraid to dive in and try to fix things. If you run into something you can't handle, check out some YouTube videos, and, as a plan B, there are always mobile RV techs that will come to you. I used to worry, "What if I take something apart and I can't get it fixed or put back together and the RV is not drivable?" Since I learned about mobile RV techs, I don't worry about this anymore.

- Don't drive too far in a day and consider staying longer when you stop. I like to drive at most about 200 to 300 miles in a day unless someone is traveling with me who can do part of the driving. I've driven further than this in a day when I'm just trying to get from point A to point B, but if you want to enjoy your trip, don't wear yourself out driving. And by all means, plan to arrive well before dark.
- Don't spend a lot of money on solar to start with. If you don't have a generator, you can get one for $700 to $1,000 if you're going to be doing much boondocking. Honda makes a great little one that's very quiet. Later, if you find out you need solar or more solar panels and batteries, then you can invest in solar. Solar is great if you use it, but you can sink a lot of money in solar and then find that you're not really using the system.
- Learn to drive your rig. Whether you have a camper or a motorhome, consider taking a driving course. At the very least, watch some YouTube videos about how to back your rig, how to downshift, and how to tow if you're towing a car or a trailer.
- The world is not as scary as you imagine. Most people you meet are nice, friendly, honest, caring, and helpful. There's no riff-raff around RV parks or in the boondocks where you decide to park. Don't be afraid of the

unknown. Crooks and thieves know that there are slim pickings in an RV. There are no valuables, and no cash. What could they steal?

- Don't rush things. Go slow. You have nowhere to go and you have all day to get there. Also, go slow when you're looking for an RV to buy, dumping your tanks, backing into a campsite, getting ready to pull out of a campsite, and on and on. Go slow. Don't rush. Mistakes happen when you rush.
- When you're just making miles and going from point A to point B, you can boondock at Walmart, Cracker Barrel, Cabela's, HarvestHost.com locations, etc. These are great places to spend the night—and they're free. The first time you do it, it will probably feel weird, but experienced RVers do it all the time. I was at a Walmart recently and there were over 40 other RVers spending the night there. Of course, check with the manager and get permission.
- The indicator lights that tell you how full your black tank, gray water, and fresh water tanks are not reliable. The sensors get contaminated. They will sometimes read full or half-full after you've just dumped your tanks. I have an external monitoring system (sensors that stick on the outside of the tanks) that work great, but you don't have to spend the money on a system like this.

You will soon learn how to know how full each tank is. Just don't trust your indicator lights.

- About every three months put a cup of chlorine bleach in your fresh water tank, fill your tank and drive around for a few minutes to let it slosh around as you drive, and then open each faucet and run water until you smell chlorine (be sure to run some water through your water heater. Let it set overnight and then drain all of the water out of your tanks. After that, refill your holding tank and flush it out again. Be sure to turn each faucet on and flush the chlorine water out of the lines. You may have to do this two or more times to get rid of the chlorine smell. Now you have clean, safe, fresh water.
- Leave some wiggle room in your travel plans.
- I wish I had started keeping a journal earlier. I keep one now, but I wish I had started sooner. What was the couple's names you met at the last campground? What was the name of the campground by the river? What was the name of that restaurant that had the great lasagna? You might think you won't forget these things, but, after a while, everything starts running together. Keeping a journal will pay off big time.
- Have multiple sources of income. Almost everyone I meet in the RVing community has more than one

source of income. Even if they don't need the money, they like to dabble in something. It's just a fact of life. You need to have more than one source of income.

- Have an emergency fund. Don't spend all your cash on buying the best RV you can afford. You never know when a tire will blow out, when you'll have a wreck and have to pay a deductible, or when you will need some expensive repairs. Having an emergency fund will give you peace of mind. Ideally, you should be adding to your emergency fund. The best way to add to your emergency fund is to pick up other sources of income. You can always cut expenses a little (eating out less, boondocking more, etc.), but to make major progress on building your emergency fund, find a way to have an additional source of income. See Chapter 15.
- Be prepared for maintenance problems with your RV—even if it's a new one. In fact, if it's a new RV, you will have even more maintenance problems. The problems will probably be covered under warranty if you have a new RV, but there will be more of them. One of the advantages of buying a new car is that you can expect not to have to deal with maintenance problems for a while. That's not the case with RVs. The difference is that cars are built on an assembly line. RVs are not.

- I wish I had known more about boondocking, how to do it, where to do it, etc. Most RVers end up doing some boondocking and some RVers boondock almost exclusively. You can learn as you go, but spend some time reading books, watching YouTube videos, and reading some blogs and you can learn faster and end up saving a lot of money. The only thing you can't learn without trial and error is whether you'll like it or not, but, for sure, you'll like it better if you're prepared and if you know what to expect and know what you're doing. I had been RVing for over a year before I ever heard of the concept of parking overnight in Walmart parking lots. If I had known this earlier, it would have saved me a lot of money and a lot of time and trouble when I was traveling.

- When you're staying in RV parks, you can save a lot by staying for a month at a time. The monthly rate is about the same as the cost of staying for two weeks. In other words, the monthly rate is approximately twice the weekly rate. There are a lot of other advantages to staying somewhere for a month or longer. For one thing, you get to know and experience the area. When you're boondocking, remember that a lot of state and national parks and national forests have a 14-day limit, so you must move around.

- Leaving your job, home, community, and friends all at one time can be stressful, but it can also be liberating.
- If you have kids and are going to be home-schooling them, do your homework. Home-schooling is legal in every state, but the rules vary a lot. You can learn the laws for each state and a lot more about home-schooling at this website: **https://hslda.org/content**
- Also check out **www.FulltimeFamilies.com**.
- Have a set of big, over the ear, headphones for each person.
- Watch some videos on backing a motorhome or camper, and also learn the proper hand signals. Note: Tell the driver which way the back of the RV should go. Do NOT tell them which way to turn the steering wheel. You will look much more like an experienced RVer if you don't try to tell the driver which way to turn the steering wheel.
- I wish I had known how much I enjoy staying in one location for extended periods of time. All the RVing YouTube videos make it sound like RVers only stay in a place for a few days at a time. Some of them do, but I've found that I like to get to know a place.
- RVers are very friendly, but you must make an effort to meet people. Plan on attending rallies. Attend an FMCA,

Escapees, or Xscapers rally and you'll be sure to meet like-minded RVers.

- Learning and growing is part of the RVing adventure.
- Get rid of stress. Even if you're working while you're living in your RV, you don't have to be productive all the time. When you eliminate stress, you may notice that a lot of your health problems go away. Stress is very hard on your body.
- If you have teenage kids, it might be a good idea to consider where they want to attend college. If you set up your domicile state as a state where they want to attend a state university, the kids can end up paying in-state tuition instead of out-of-state tuition. Of course, kids change their minds, and you know what they say about the best laid plans of mice and men. But it's something to think about and consider.
- Just because you have read something doesn't mean you will know it or remember it, so plan on referring to sections of this book from time to time. Heck, I often refer to sections of my books from time to time, and I wrote the books.
- Realize that RVing will change you. You will never be the same. Your eyes will have been opened to a whole new world. You may hang up the keys one day, but when you do, you can say, "I lived my dream." People

ask me what I'm going to do when I get too old to drive my car, I tell them I'm going to put it behind my motorhome and tow it.

- This is a unique time in history. Enjoy the adventure.

Bottom line—what I wish I had known 7 years ago: A few of these "RVing words of wisdom" as I called them are things that I wish I had known before I started RVing, but many of them are just important things that I wanted to make sure you were aware of.

Chapter 15

You Need a Source of Income

"Every man dies. Not every man really lives."

~ William Wallace

You may not need a source of income, but many RVers do—even if they're retired. And even if you don't need a source of income, having extra money coming in is always nice.

Also, having a money-making project to work on can be interesting and enjoyable.

Back when I was getting ready to start living full-time in an RV, I wish I had known how easy it would be to make money while being on the road.

The biggest concern I had when I was considering living full time in an RV was whether I could I make enough money to support the lifestyle without dipping into my savings and investments. I wasn't concerned about whether I would like the lifestyle or not.

I know a lot of people who are thinking about venturing out on the RVing lifestyle are concerned about whether they will like it or not and what they will do if they don't like the lifestyle. That wasn't a concern for me. I was sure I would love the lifestyle, and I was right.

I was already more or less retired, but I was still dabbling in money-making projects. I was working with restaurants and hotels on their marketing projects along with selling some items on the internet. And I had my Social Security income.

I was pretty sure I could get by, but it wouldn't be easy to continue selling things on the internet when I was on the road (where would I store things?). And it wouldn't be easy to work with hotels and restaurants if I wasn't around much.

I think it was kind of like the feeling people experience when they consider quitting their jobs. I would be walking away from my side-hustle that I was using to supplement my Social Security income.

I wish I had known how easy it would be to make money living full time in an RV

I didn't know anyone who was living in an RV and making money while they were doing it. I didn't know about the many options that were available to me.

I had heard about what is called "workamping" where RVers worked as camp hosts or worked in the campground office in exchange for free camping, but most of them were not making any money—just getting free camping. I had not heard of working for Amazon for a few months a year during the pre-Christmas rush and making money. I now know that a lot of RVers do this. It's one of the best paying gigs for RVers.

There were plenty of options available to make money on the road, and a lot of people were doing it. I just didn't know about any of them.

Now there are a lot of blogs and YouTube videos with people explaining how they make money while they're on the road. And to make things even better, there are way more opportunities available now than there were seven years ago.

In addition to all the ways RVers are making money while they're on the road, I've found a lot of RVers who are making money in ways they had not planned on. You could say that the money (or the opportunity to make money) just fell out of the sky. Not really, but they are making money in ways they had not even thought of when they hit the road. Here are two examples:

Example 1:

Nathan and Marissa of Less Junk, More Journey—Youtube.com/channel/UC2IENUorXc6kRtIiAGPRKZA had no experience of or interest in shooting and editing videos when they hit the road full-time. But now with their YouTube channel, Less Junk, More Journey, (which has over 105,000 subscribers) they're posting several videos a week and this project mostly supports their full-time RV lifestyle. Check them out. I love their videos.

Example 2:

I'm an engineer. I don't know anything about writing. I had never gotten anything better than a "C" out of an English class in college in my life. Now I have written 13 books. The income from the sale of these books pays for my RVing lifestyle and allows me to add to my savings. When I started RVing full time, I had never even considered the concept of making a living writing books.

The internet has opened up a whole new world of ways RVers can make money while living on the road, but even without the internet, there are hundreds of ways RVers are making money.

In previous books I have written a whole chapter on how RVers are making money on the road, but a chapter doesn't even scratch the surface of how to make money while living in an RV.

I find new ways all the time that RVers are using to make a living while on the road. I could add a lot to what I've already written, but I decided I would still only be giving you a glimpse of how to make money on the road.

There's a new book out by Bill Myers called *Road Cash—How to make money while living on the road.* You can get the eBook version of this book on Amazon for $3.99 at the link below:

Amazon.com/dp/B0721832MD

There is also a printed version of the book available. If you have any interest at all in making money while living on the road, you need this book. You'll be amazed at the options that are available for making an income while living in your RV. This book is not theory. The techniques described in this book are being used by RVers to support their lifestyle.

Bottom line—what I wish I had known 7 years ago: In a nutshell, I wish I had known how easy it would be to make money living full-time in an RV.

Chapter 16

Summing It All Up

"Do not follow where the path may lead. Go instead where there is no path and leave a trail."

~ Ralph Waldo Emerson

Since you've read this far in this book, you've learned a lot about the RVing lifestyle and for sure you know the things I wish I had known before I hit the road seven years ago.

You may not have the answers to all your questions, but, hopefully, for the questions you still have I have pointed you in a direction that will allow you to find the answers you're looking for.

One of the best sources of additional information is to watch the YouTube videos that I've linked to in the previous chapters and the links in Chapter 17 describing *Other Resources*.

You can also find additional information about specific RVing topics in one of my 12 other books about RVing. The books are listed in the back of this book and on my website, **www.LifeRV.com**.

I'm not trying to push my other books (oh wait, yes, I am).

Keep in mind you don't have to have all the answers. Accept the fact that every decision you make for the rest of your life will be made with incomplete information.

Make a decision and carve it in Jell-O. In other words, consider the fact that your plans are shaky.

After all, if there were no unknowns, there would be no adventure.

One of the many things I love about my RVing lifestyle is that I'm always around people (old and young) who are making decisions, making things happen, and doing things. My life is never boring. Your life won't be boring either when you start RVing.

Hopefully, now that you've read this book, you have your dream clearly defined, you know what you want to do, and you know how to make it happen.

My guess is that you want to get rid of your stuff, hit the road, live the RV lifestyle, and never look back.

If that doesn't describe you, then you probably stopped reading this book way before you got to this point.

A final thought about choosing the RVing lifestyle

Making this big of a change in your life will result in an upheaval of everything you know. There will be risks. Accept the risks as normal and go on with your life.

As of now, adventure is in your blood. I think your decision has already been made, so set a date and make it happen. The timing will never be perfect, so make it happen now, and start enjoying your new lifestyle.

Hit the road and soak in whatever slice of nature you can. Breathe in deeply and experience the calm of the wilderness (a wilderness is anywhere that's new to you). Feel renewed and live a life with no stress. What are you waiting for?

You may not live the RVing lifestyle forever, but when you hang up the keys, you can look back and say, "I lived my dream."

If you have any questions for me, feel free to email me at

Jminchey@gmail.com

I would love to hear from you. Also, check out my website at www.LifeRV.com

Bottom line—what I wish I had known 7 years ago: This whole book is about the things I wish I had known before I started RVing seven years ago. Obviously, you don't have to know these things, because I didn't know them, and I survived, had a great time, and didn't experience any financial disasters.

However, if I had known these things, I would have saved some money, avoided some stress, and possibly enjoyed RV life even more. I'm sure I'll learn even more things during my next seven years on the road.

Chapter 17

Other Resources

"If you are going through hell, keep going."

~ Winston Churchill

This chapter contains information on resources that I think you will find helpful. Many of these links and resources have been pointed out previously in different parts of the book, but I'm including them here so you will have what I consider to be the most useful references all in one place.

I have placed the links in categories. Some of the links could fit into more than one category, but I have tried to put them in the category they best fit in. You will find a few of the links listed in more than one category. I did this in order to make the categories more comprehensive.

Blogs I follow

LessJunkMoreJourney.com –Nathan and Marissa publish one of my favorite blogs.

They also post new YouTube videos five days a week. Subscribe to their YouTube Channel to be notified when new videos are posted.

They are a young couple who sold everything and now live full time in an RV with their four-year-old little girl (and another kid is on the way).

Technomadia.com – Cherie and Chris have been full-time RVing for over 10 years. They say a technomadia is a technology-enabled nomad. That's where the name of their website came from. They travel in a very fancy converted bus that they have geeked-out. Their site is a wealth of information for all aspects of RVing and especially for anything to do with technology or traveling. They have written a great book, *The Mobile Internet Handbook*, which is the Bible when it comes to getting connected to the Internet while on the road. They update the book often. You can find this book (and their other books and apps) on their website and on Amazon. (Note: They now live part of the year in their motorhome and part of the year on their boat.)

Wheelingit.us – Nina and Paul Wheeling travel in a 40-foot Class A motorhome. Nina writes one of the most information-rich blogs on the Internet. They do a lot of boondocking and she writes some wonderful blog posts on boondocking as well as traveling and other RVing subjects. (Update: As of 2019 they have now sold their motorhome and moved to France, but now they have bought another motorhome and are RVing in Europe.)

GoneWithTheWynns.net – Nikki and Jason Wynn sold everything, bought an RV and off they went to discover the world—at least the part they could get to in their motorhome. They provide a lot of great articles and entertaining, high-quality videos that cover their travels, equipment, and all aspects of RVing.

(Update: As of October 2017 they have sold their motorhome and bought a catamaran sailboat and are living full time on their sailboat, sailing around the world.) They add a lot of articles and videos now about sailing, but the vast archives of RVing articles and videos on their website are well worth looking at. Reading their blog is fun, enjoyable, and informative. You'll love it.

Interstellarorchard.com – Becky Schade is in her mid-30s, college educated, and a single, female RVer who has been living full time in her 17-foot Casita camper for almost five years. (Update: As of 2019 she has sold her "big" 17-foot camper and now lives in a 13-foot teardrop camper.) She lives on a very tight budget and pays for her lifestyle by doing workamping at Amazon, working at national parks, and sometimes she does other gigs. She also supplements her income by writing. Her book, *Solo Full-time RVing on a Budget – Go Small, Go Now,* is a great book if you're on a tight budget and looking to get started RVing. You can find the book on her website and on Amazon. When you visit her website, be sure to click on the link to "*Start here*" in the top navigation bar. It is useful stuff. She has a new book out now, *The Little Guide to Dreaming BIG.*

CheapRVLiving.com – Bob Wells has been living in a van for 15 years. He boondocks most of the time and lives mainly off of his Social Security income plus income from writing, and occasionally he does some workamping jobs as a camp host. In addition to explaining how he lives, he also writes some great blog posts (that include wonderful pictures) about his travels and where he's camping. He also posts some interesting videos on his YouTube channel. He also posts videos where he interviews other full-time RVers.

GoSmallLiveLarge.com – Scott has a blog and a video channel that you'll find interesting. You can find links to his videos on his website. His blog and videos are about traveling and living full time in his van as a digital nomad, solo RVer.

Blog.Feedspot.com/rv_blogs – You can learn a lot from blogs and if you want to follow even more blogs than the ones I've listed here, this link will take you to a list of what is called the "Top 100 RV Blogs."

This website also provides a brief description of each of the blogs. I don't follow all 100 of these blogs—if I did, I wouldn't have time to do anything else. Take a look at the list and see if any of them look interesting to you. My guess is you'll find some you like.

RV forums

Reading forums is a great way to learn about RVing. You can see what questions other RVers are asking (and see the answers being posted by fellow RVers). You can also get answers to your own questions. Here are the three popular RV forums I follow almost every day.

RV.net/forum – Note that this website has a dot-**net** and not a dot-**com** suffix. The discussion group is broken into several categories—Class A, Fifth wheels, Workamping, etc. Check out the different discussion groups and you will learn a lot. I check into these forums almost daily.

RV-dreams.ActiveBoard.com –This is an active discussion forum with the discussions sorted by topics. Check out the *Community Chat* section, the *Buying an RV*, and the

RV Maintenance sections or others that look interesting to you.

iRV2.com/forums – This is another active RVing forum that I check frequently.

Other RVing Forums – In addition to the popular forums listed above, there are forums for just about every brand and type of RV (Roadtrek, Airstream, National, Casita, Fleetwood, Forest River, Tiffin, etc.). Search Google and find the forum for your rig. It will be a great place to get answers to the many questions you will have about your RV. For example, "Where is the fuse for the water pump?" Your manual may not tell you, but someone on the forum for your type of RV will know and tell you almost immediately.

Finding campgrounds

Sometimes I pay full price for a campsite, but most of the time I get discounts of 50% or more. There are two main ways I get the 50% discounts. First, I can almost always get discounts of 50% or more by booking a campsite for a month at a time. That's what I usually do. The second way I get the 50% discounts is by using one of the websites or apps below:

PassportAmerica.com – Membership is $44 a year and you get a 50% discount at 1,900 campgrounds all around the country. Stay two or three nights and you've paid for your whole year's membership. I consider being a member of Passport America one of the best investments in the RV world.

AllStays.com – This site has a lot of campground and travel information. You can also get their information as an app at AllStays.com/apps.

RVparking.com – This site has reviews and recommendations for 19,000 campgrounds. One thing I like about this site is that you get to see why people like or dislike a particular campground.

OvernightRVparking.com – Membership is $24.95 a year. They have the web's largest database of free RV parking locations in the US and Canada. Their database contains 13,922 RV Parking and No Parking locations in the USA and Canada. Search by your current location, city and state or province or zip code. Download PDF files by state or province.

UltimateCampgrounds.com – This site provides comprehensive information on over 31,000 public campgrounds of all types in the US and Canada. They also have an app.

America the Beautiful Senior Pass – If you're 62 or older and are a US citizen, you can purchase the *America the Beautiful National Parks and Federal Recreational Lands Pass.* It's also called the *Senior Pass.* It's $80 for a lifetime membership if you buy it in person or $90 if you want to receive it by mail. It allows you free admission and discount camping (which is usually a 50% discount).

If you're not 62, you can get the Annual Pass with the same benefits.

You can get either one of the passes by mail by going to this website:

store.usgs.gov/pass/senior.html

To find locations where you can get the pass in person, go to:

store.usgs.gov/pass/PassIssuanceList.pdf

I recently camped at Curtis Creek campground in the Pisgah National Forest in North Carolina. There were 14 campsites there and only two of them were occupied. With the pass the cost was only $2.50 a night to camp and enjoy some of the most beautiful views in the North Carolina Mountains. You have to go about three miles up the mountain on a gravel road, but there is no problem getting a Class A motorhome to the campground.

FreeCampsites.net – This is a free website that allows you to search for free camping places. You can enter a city and state or a zip code and see a map showing free camping places. In most cases, there is information about each site in addition to its location.

HarvestHosts.com – This is a great resource for finding farms and wineries all over the country where you can camp overnight for free. Staying overnight at a winery or farm is a fun experience. Membership is $79 a year. I find it well worth the membership fee. Harvest Hosts provides you the opportunity to travel to new areas, have unique experiences and enjoy purchasing locally grown and produced products. (You are expected to buy a bottle or two of wine or some fruits or vegetables.) They have over 600 locations for you to camp free.

CasinoCamper.net – Most casinos will allow you to camp overnight and many of them will even give you some free chips (they want to get you inside, so you will start gambling). If your luck is like mine, this option might end up costing you more than just paying to camp at an RV park.

Walmart – Most people don't think of Walmart as an RV park, but most Walmart stores allow RVers free overnight parking. Remember that you are parking and not camping, so don't put your slides out, lower your jacks, bring out your grill or run your generator.

BoondockersWelcome.com – This website lists hundreds of places where you can boondock free of charge. You will generally be camping in other RVers' driveways. It's $24.95 a year if you will only be a guest and $19.95 if you have a place and agree to also let RVers camp free in your driveway.

When you agree to be a host and let people boondock in your driveway, they don't just show up. They contact you and get permission. You only let people boondock at your place when it's convenient for you. If you're going to be out of town or having company, you probably don't want boondockers during that time.

I haven't used this website yet, but everyone I've talked to who has used it said they had a wonderful experience when they did. The hosts are friendly, gracious, and happy to have you. They like to have fellow RVers to talk to and visit with.

RVing videos I like

Search YouTube for the word "RV" and you will find five million videos. Some are extremely useful and informative; some contain bad and untrue information. Some are interesting and entertaining, and some are just plain boring.

I haven't watched all five million of the videos, but I have watched a lot of them (and I do mean a lot). I usually watch a few every day. Below are some of the videos I consider to be worth your time to watch. Turn off the TV and spend an hour or so watching these videos and you will be entertained and informed.

Many of the videos I have linked to here have been linked to previously in other chapters. I'm providing the links here, so you will have what I consider to be the most important RV videos in one place.

Note #1. I have watched a lot of YouTube videos, and one thing I've found is that on most videos I can speed them up to 1.5x the speed and still understand what's being said. This allows me to watch more videos in the time I've set aside to watch YouTube videos. To do this, click on the little gear symbol in the bottom right corner of the video and then click on "Speed." A pop-up menu will appear. Click on 1.5 and see how you like it.

Note #2. When you're watching these videos, you will see other videos on the page by the same people or about the same topic. Check out some of these. Watching YouTube videos about RVing is an entertaining way to quickly learn a lot about RVs and the RVing lifestyle.

Now I'll get on with the list of videos:

Vimeo.com/71385845 – I love this 7-minute video. It's about a young couple and their full-time RVing adventure traveling with a small child. Take a look at it. I think you'll like it.

YouTube.com/watch?v=NGxmSGf2Kr8 – This 14-minute video shows 17 full-time RVers as they describe how they make a living while living the RVing lifestyle. If you're looking to make some extra money while you enjoy RVing, maybe you can get some ideas from these RVers.

YouTube.com/watch?v=g0UJAMNXJbk – This 8-minute video is an interview with a retired couple describing their life on the road and how and why they decided to make the transition to the full-time RVing lifestyle.

YouTube.com/watch?v=jAhBnq2pLNk – This is another 8-minute video interview with a retired couple.

YouTube.com/watch?v=ebbo800_Rg0 – This 11-minute video interview is with a young, single, female RVer. If you're thinking about being a solo RVer, I think you will find her story interesting. By the way, she has now been on the road for seven years and still loves the lifestyle.

YouTube.com/watch?v=E6_AYrdfDS0 – Nathan and Marissa have had four RVs in three years, and in this video, they talk about what they wish they had known before they started their RVing life. (Note: Since this video was posted, they have changed from a Class A motorhome to an Airstream travel trailer.)

YouTube.com/results?search_query=rvgeeks – This is a link to a list of how-to RV videos by RV Geeks. You will find a lot of useful information in these videos.

YouTube.com/watch?v=7AR4uOmGfxc – This is a link to one of Kyle and Olivia's *Drivin' and Vivin'* Q&A videos.

They are a young couple living full time in their tiny camper. Check out several of their videos. I think you will find them interesting. They are now in the process of renovating a larger Airstream camper.

YouTube.com/watch?v=BsEs-CLBbaU&t=98s – Marc and Tricia travel with their three kids and a golden retriever. They have posted several fun, interesting, and informative RVing videos.

YouTube.com/watch?v=c2xkfkhfcEg – Nate and Christian Axness are a young couple who travel with their two kids. I think you will find their videos interesting.

TechNomadia.com/ramblings – If you like interview style videos, this link will take you to dozens of these videos produced by Chris and Cherie at Technomadia.com.

YouTube.com/watch?v=bkiK5ZUgLT8 – Here is a short 40-second video by Pippi Peterson. She is a young, single female who lives and travels full time in her 1992 Class A motorhome. She posts a new video every week about her RV life on the road, and, believe it or not, about RV maintenance and modifications that she does herself. Update: She has now sold her Class A motorhome and is RVing in a fifth wheel.

YouTube.com/watch?v=xsiLyjgQyzE – In 2012, Lidia bought a 28-foot Class C motorhome and hit the road with her 10-year-old son. She later changed to a 28-foot travel trailer and then a truck camper. This video explains why she likes the truck camper the best. Her son is now 17 and she has bought (and is renovating) an Airstream for him.

YouTube.com/watch?v=xoy3vNUjLOU – Carolyn is a 50-year-old, single woman who quit her high-paying corporate job and now lives full-time in her 29-foot Class C motorhome. In this video she explains why she decided to change her lifestyle.

RVing Books I like

With most eBooks priced at $2.99 to $3.99, you can get a lot of RVing information for very little money. Here are some of my favorite RVing books.

(Note: Many of these books have been linked to in previous chapters.)

Buying a Used Motorhome – How to get the most for your money and not get burned by Bill Myers.

Don't even think about buying a motorhome without reading this book. The information in this book saved me thousands of dollars. And, more importantly, it helped me pick the right motorhome for my needs and budget.

The book is about buying a used motorhome, but a lot of the information would also be useful and helpful if you were considering buying a travel trailer or fifth wheel camper. You can find the book on Amazon at this link:

Amazon.com/dp/B007OV4TBY

Solo Full-time RVing on a Budget – Go Small, Go Now by Becky Schade. You can find the book on Amazon at this link:

Amazon.com/dp/B00W30OFCE

Or you can find it on her website at

InterstellarOrchard.com

She has another book, *The Little Guide to Dreaming BIG.* You can find it at this link:

Amazon.com/dp/B01HREJMZK

Road Cash – This book shows you dozens of step-by-step ways RVers are making money while living on the road. I just finished reading it and it's excellent. I have already been using some of the techniques discussed, and they work just as described. There are many other location-independent, income-producing methods described that I'm eager to implement. This is one of the many books by William Myers. Here's a link to the book on Amazon:

Amazon.com/dp/B0721832MD

The Mobile Internet Handbook - For US Based RVers, Cruisers & Nomads (2018 version) – This comprehensive guide to mobile internet options for US-based RVers was written by full-time RVing technomads Chris and Cherie. You can get the book on Amazon at this link:

Amazon.com/dp/B079JW8W69

Convert Your Minivan into a Mini RV Camper by William H. Myers. For $200 to $300 and a minivan, you can have an RV that you can comfortably live in. You can find the book on Amazon at this link:

Amazon.com/dp/1530265126

How to Live in a Car, Van, or RV: And Get Out of Debt, Travel, and Find True Freedom by Bob Wells. You can find the book on Amazon at this link:

Amazon.com/dp/1479215889

RV Basic Training Manual – Motorhome Driving Course. Learn what every commercial driver MUST know and every RV driver SHOULD know. The book is a little pricey at $30 but well worth it. It's a 46-page manual with a lot of pictures and drawings, so it's easy to read. You can order it at this website:

RvBasicTraining.com/buy-manual.html

Get What's Yours – The secrets to Maxing Out Your Social Security by Laurence J. Kotlikoff and Philip Moeller. The book has been revised to cover the new laws. You can get the book from Amazon at:

Amazon.com/dp/B00LD1OPP6

This is the 12th book I've written about the different aspects of RVing. You can find a complete list of my RVing books on the right panel of my website at www.**LifeRV.com** or look at the last two pages of this book for a list. They are all available on Amazon.

RVing novels

If you're looking for some great novels with plots built around RVing, I would recommend the Mango Bob series. The series includes *Mango Bob, Mango Lucky, Mango Bay, Mango Glades, Mango Key, Mango Blues,* and *Mango Digger.*

They all revolve around a 35-year-old single guy and his adventures as he lives and travels around Florida in his motorhome. I have read all of the books in this series and I love them. I think my favorite is the last one, *Mango Digger.* I really liked *Mango Glades* too. It's hard to pick a favorite. I liked them all. A new one will be coming out soon.

You can find them on Amazon at this link:

Amazon.com/dp/1889562033

RVing groups

Escapees.com – I recommend joining this group. It's $39.95 a year and you also get membership in the new Xscapers.com group (which is for younger RVers) at no extra charge. With your membership you will receive their printed magazine every other month. I consider this the most useful RVing magazine in the industry. They also offer discounts on insurance, camping, and a lot of other things I spend money on. Take a look at their website and see if you think what they offer would be useful to you.

RVillage.com – This is a free website and it's a great way to keep up with where your RVing friends are and let them know where you are.

FMCA.com – The Family Motor Coach Association is a popular group with RVers. The organization has been around for a long time. Take a look at their website and the benefits they offer. The cost is $50 for the first year and $40 for renewals. One of the things they offer is a program for getting great discounts on Michelin tires. They also host awesome RVing rallies. There were over 3,000 RVers at one of their recent rallies.

Getting healthcare on the road is changing

Important note: How the government will be changing healthcare options is totally unknown right now. I'm sure there will be changes in 2019, so be sure to check the six websites listed below to get the latest information.

- **RverInsurance.com**
- **RverHIExchange.com**
- **HealthSherpa.com**
- **RVerInsurance.com**
- **Teladoc.com** – 24/7 access to a doctor, by phone
- **24-7HealthInsurance.com**
- **Kff.org/interactive/subsidy-calculator** – This is a link to a website that has a handy tool to provide estimates of health insurance premiums and subsidies for people purchasing insurance on their own in health insurance exchanges created by the ACA (Affordable Care Act). It will most likely be updated to include information on new programs that become available. Check it out.

How to find work as an RVer

If you're RVing full time or thinking about it and want to do some part-time work while you're RVing, the websites below will be useful to you.

CoolWorks.com – This is a free site.

CoolWorks.com/jobs-with-rv-spaces – This link goes directly to a page on the above website that probably has what you're looking for.

Workamper.com – This is a subscription website. The cost is $47 a year for the Diamond Plan.

Work-for-Rvers-and-Campers.com

Apps

AllStays.com/apps/camprv.htm – This is the app I use the most. With this app I can find reviews of almost 30,000 campgrounds, find locations of dump stations, find overhead clearances, and even find grades on steep mountain roads. It costs $9.99 to download the app to your iPhone or Android device.

Google Maps – In my opinion Google Maps is more accurate than Apple Maps, and it's free.

RVParking.com – This app contains almost a quarter of a million reviews of 20,000 campgrounds. The price is right for this app—it's free.

US Public Lands: You can find information about public lands with this app:

TwoStepsBeyond.com/apps/USPublicLands

About 47% of the land in the western part of the US is owned by the government. If you've ever wanted to know where to camp free on government land, you'll love this app. This app shows BLM, Forest Service, NPS, and public land boundary maps. You can download the app from Google Play or iTunes.

Reserve.WanderingLabs.com – When you check for availability at a campground and there's no campsite available on the dates you want to camp, instead of checking back every few days, let this app do it for you. Instead of checking back every few days, it will check every few minutes and send you an email as soon as a space becomes available.

The app is free, but if you want to make a small donation, you can get the version that checks constantly instead of every few minutes.

Waze.com – Your smartphone can be a reasonable substitute for an RVer specific GPS. By RVer specific GPS I mean one that gives you information about bridge clearances, grades, dump stations, etc.

Having a hands-free phone holder in the RV is key for this.

This app also has real-time info on road conditions, traffic backups, and speed traps. It's called Waze. You can download it at Waze.com. I really like it. The price is right too—it's free.

Copilotgps.com/en-us/rv-navigation – Don't pay $300 to $500 for a GPS device with all the information RVers need. You can get this app that will turn your phone into GPS especially for RVs for $39.99.

GasBuddy.com – Find the lowest price on gas wherever you are, and it's free.

Snapseed – Easy and simple basic photo editing while you travel. You can download it on your computer or download the app for your phone.

Other websites

Spend an evening or two reading the articles and watching the videos you'll find on the websites listed below and you'll know more about RVing than most of the RVers out there. Best of all, I think you'll find the way the information is presented in these videos, blogs, and articles to be enjoyable and entertaining.

I check these websites for new information at least once a week. Most of them have a way to sign up and get an email message when new information is posted.

Technomadia.com – Chris and Cherie have been full-time RVers for more than 10 years. They share a lot of useful information on their site. They have a big converted bus that they have done wonders with and made it fancy and functional. Spend some time on their website, and you will soon know a lot more than most long-time RVers. New articles are posted every week, and there are a lot of video interviews on this site that you will find interesting. Note: They now spend half of their time living and traveling on their boat.

RV-Dreams.com – Howard and Linda have a website that's full of information and personal experiences. Turn the TV off and spend a night reading and absorbing the wealth of information they have to offer. There is also a lively discussion forum on the site. You can find a link to their discussion forum in the left nav panel on their site. Howard quit being an attorney several years ago and they hit the road and became full-time RVers.

InterstellarOrchard.com – Becky Schade is a 35-year-old, college educated, single female living full time in her RV. She does workamping and writing to fund her travels. On her site, you can read her articles, and you can learn more about what she does and her solo RVing lifestyle. She posts a couple of new articles every week and I think you will find them enlightening and interesting. Some of her articles are about her travels, and some are about what she does, what she thinks, and her life in general on the road as a full-time single, female RVer.

CheapRvLiving.com – Bob Wells has a ton of information on his website about living in a van. He has lived in it full time and traveled for many years. He lives mostly on his Social Security. Check out his website and see how he does it.

Motorhome.com/download-dinghy-guides – Some cars can be towed with all four wheels down and some require that you use a dolly. At this site, for $1.99, they offer a downloadable guide. They have a different guide for each model year. If you already own a car that you're considering towing, be sure to check your car's owner's manual to see if it can be towed with all four wheels down.

PplMotorhomes.com/sold/soldmenu.htm – This site tells you what RVs have recently sold for. The people at PPL Motorhomes sell about 4,000 motorhomes a year, and they show you what each one actually sold for. They also always have a huge inventory of used RVs for sale. Most of them are on consignment.

RVSchool.com – This is a great RV driving school. They teach you to drive in your own motorhome. Take a look at their schedule and see if they're going to be offering training at a rally near you. They offer discounts at most RV rallies.

Use **Yelp.com** to find recommended local services—dentists, restaurants, auto repair shops, computer repair shops, etc.

There are thousands of good sources of information on the internet (and, of course, thousands of sites with information that's not so useful). The links I have provided in this chapter are to the RVing resources (books, forums, videos, apps, and websites) that I use the most and the ones I think provide really useful and trusted information. I highly recommend you take a look at all of the resources I have linked to in this chapter and throughout the book.

If you have questions for me, feel free to email me at **Jminchey@gmail.com** or go to my website at **LifeRV.com** to learn more about the RV lifestyle and adventure. On the website, you can post your questions in the discussion forum and you will get answers from me and other RVers.

Whether you enjoy the RVing adventure or whether you find it frustrating will be determined a lot by your attitude. Spend some time watching the videos and reading the blogs I've linked to in this chapter, and I think when you realize how much fun other RVers are having and how much they are enjoying the adventure, it will help you realize how wonderful this lifestyle can be.

If you're considering becoming an RVer, realize that there is a lot to learn in order to safely and economically enjoy the RV lifestyle. Check out the links in this chapter, and you will be well on your way to becoming an informed and experienced RVer.

Bottom line—what I wish I had known 7 years ago: For sure I wish I had known about all the resources I've linked to in this chapter. The information in the links provided in this chapter is worth its weight in gold. I refer to some of these links almost every day for something.

Did You Like This Book?

I hope this information has been helpful. I've tried to explain things in the simplest way possible. If you think I've over simplified some things, it's because I'm a simple man and I like to follow Albert Einstein's philosophy.

"If you can't explain it to a six-year-old, you don't understand it yourself."

~ Albert Einstein

If you have any questions for me, feel free to email me at

Jminchey@gmail.com

I would love to hear from you.

I need your help

If you liked this book, I need your help.

I would appreciate it if you would take a minute to leave a review on Amazon. (You really can do it in only one minute.)

Writing a review is not like writing a high school book report. All you need to do is write a sentence or two saying that you liked the book.

Thank you,

Jerry Minchey

P.S. On the following pages are some of my other books that you might find interesting and entertaining.

(You can find them on Amazon.)

Other books by the author available on Amazon

More books by the author available on Amazon

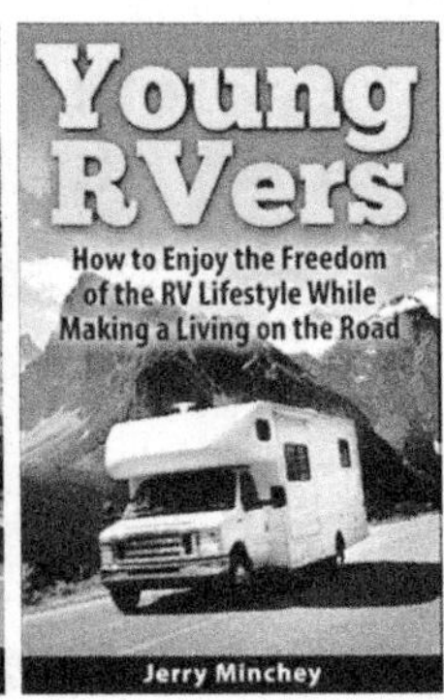

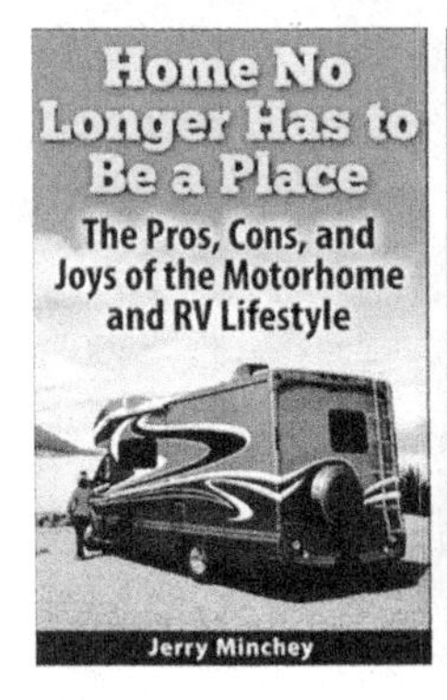

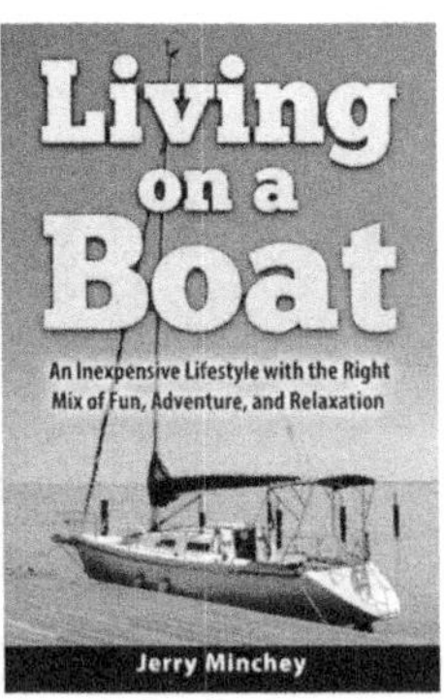

Made in the USA
Coppell, TX
23 February 2021